THE ORIGINS
CHINESE
KONGSI

WANG TAI PENG

THE ORIGINS OF CHINESE KONGSI

Pelanduk
Publications

Published by
Pelanduk Publications (M) Sdn Bhd
24 Jalan 20/16A, 46300 Petaling Jaya
Selangor Darul Ehsan
Malaysia.

Perpustakaan Negara Malaysia
Cataloguing-In-Publication Data

Wang, Tai Peng
The Origins of Chinese Kongsi/Wang Tai Peng
Bibliography: p.115-120
Includes index
1. Triads (Gangs) – China – History.
2. Triads (Gangs).
3. Chinese – Social conditions.
4. Chinese – Economic conditions.
I. Title.
909.04951

ISBN 967 978 449 5

Printed by
Eagle Trading Sdn Bhd
81 Jalan SS25/32, 47301 Petaling Jaya
Selangor Darul Ehsan
Malaysia.

TABLE OF CONTENTS

ACKNOWLEDGEMENTS

Certainly in mining this piece of history, which is little known if compared with the story of western democracy, I owe a great many intellectual debts to those who have helped me.

First of all, I am indebted to Professor Wang Gungwu, not only for his useful advice in the field of Chinese and overseas Chinese history, but much more for his almost intuitive sense of terminology and the theoretical framework, which helped me to lay the foundation of this work. Equipped with an overall view, I was able to go deeper and deeper into the origins of Chinese *kongsi* which even now still lie off the beaten track of most of the historians.

Secondly, I am equally grateful to Dr Anthony Reid who paid special attention to the structure and detail of this book. The attention brought me to almost every single aspect of the life of the men of *kongsi*s, not just their government in evolution, but also their desires of earthly bliss, as towkays as well as coolies. If history is a conversation with the past, the voice from her is life.

Apart from the supervision, the help that friends generously provided me the guiding light has have been no less a contributing factor to the birth of this book. Among them: Dr Jennifer Cushman not only kindly lent me her unpublished thesis, but also painstakingly read through and commented on the first two chapters; and Dr Campbell Macknight carefully read and checked through the introduction and the last three chapters. And I am still moved by the voluntary translation of Temmink from French by Antonia Finnane, and Ian, a resident of Burton Hall, and Wendy Stoke, my Dutch tutor, and Shun Ikada for helping me with Dutch and Japanese sources.

My thanks also go to Dr Michael Stenson, Dr John Fincher, Dr Louis Sigel, Merrilyn Fitzpatrick, Christine Gee, Carol Van Beelen, who have read part of my draft. They were of additional help to me, apart from my supervisors, in checking my English and improving the flow and continuity of my prose, and in other ways such as discussion and encouragement.

To the Australian National University, I am grateful for the M.A. Scholarship which made this work possible. When it was offered two years ago in the thick of writing my M.A. Qualifying thesis it brightened my days and my work.

To my sister Wang Sin Yen who provided financial support to my first year undergraduate study at the Australian National University through her own earning and self-sacrifice, I owe her a debt that I could never repay in my life.

For the publications of this book, I must thank Prof. Khoo Kay Kim and Prof. Cheah Boon Kheng who strongly recommended it to the publisher to whom I am deeply grateful.

In using the Chinese and Japanese materials in both the Menzies Library and the National Library, the assistance given by the staff in both libraries is most appreciated.

I, of course, owe not least, a debt of gratitude to my typist, Toni Purdy, for the excellent job that she has done.

At the end, I must acknowledge the source of my interest in the history of Chinese *kongsi*. My interest in the pioneering work of Professor Lo Hsiang-lin which has been my inspiration even after all these years.

ABBREVIATIONS USED IN FOOTNOTES

CKCS   *Chung-kuo chin-shan-pai-lien she-hui ching-chi shih lun-chi* (A Symposium on the Socio-economic History of China of the Last Three Centuries), (Hong Kong, 1974), 4 vols.

CKTP   *Chung-kuo tzu-pen chu-yi meng-ya wen-ti tao-lun chi* (A Symposium on the Problems of the Sprout of Chinese Capitalism), (Peking, 1957).

HCCS   *Huang-chao ching-shih wen-pien* (Essays on Statecraft during the Ch'ing dynasty), (1873).

JSSS   *Journal of South Sea Society.*

MCSL:IP   *Ming-ch'ing shih-liao ting-pien* (Historical Materials of the Ming and Ch'ing Series B), (Shanghai, 1936 ed.).

MCSL:TP   *Ming-ch'ing shih-liao ting-pien* (Historical Materials of the Ming and Ch'ing Series D), (Taiwan, 1972 ed.).

SKYS   *Chung-kuo Chin-tai shou-kung-yeh shih tzu-liao* (Materials of the Modern History of the Chinese Handicrafts), (Peking, 1957).

SSBB   Straits Settlements Blue Book

YTCK   *Yün-nan tung-chih kao* (A General Gazetteer of Yün-nan), (1835).

SLC   *Sung-Liao-Chin She-hui Ching-chi Shih lun-chi* (A Symposium on the Socio-economic History of Sung-Liao-Chin dynasties), (Hong Kong, 1973), 2 vols.

PREFACE

About twenty years ago, Wang Tai Peng embarked on a piece of research at the Australian National University on the Chinese mining communities in West Borneo. This study took him well beyond the goldfields into many exciting and unexpected realms. The questions he asked about the nature of the Chinese 'republican government' of the late 18th and early 19th centuries (this had fascinated many European colonial officials and scholars) led him back to 15th century China, to mining enterprises in Yünnan province, to uprisings by brotherhood organizations there and in Fujian province, and even to the merchant partnerships off the South China coast which had created the maritime empires of the 17th century. The questions also led him to consider the historical place of the *kongsi*, and original political structure based on ideals of brotherhood and partnership, as a Chinese contribution to political practice, if not theory.

This work has been known to a few scholars since the author published a brief note in 1979 on the origins of the *kongsi* in the *Journal of the Malaysian Branch of the Royal Asiatic Society*. But the richness of his enquiry and argument has been buried in the library in Canberra. Only the most dedicated historians of Southeast Asia have consulted the study and they have been impressed by the value of Wang Tai Peng's research of explaining many obscure aspects of 18th and 19th century history. This recognition has encouraged the author to have his work published some 15 years after he wrote it. Because he is now a full-time journalist, he has not been able to pursue his research further and would have to be content to publish the book more or less in its original form.

When he invited me to write a preface for the book, I accepted with great pleasure. He reminded me of the years he spent pursuing the many strands of this very complex subject and discovering how more conventional historians had failed to connect these strands systematically. He may not be the first to show that various kinds of overseas Chinese organizations set up for purposes of trade, protection and management were not merely copies of earlier forms in China, but had developed out of vestiges of social practice which served to meet the alien conditions outside. But his study of the *kongsi* demonstrates that this is the most ingenious type of brotherhood-partnership structure to be used as a system of government anywhere in the world. How this institution was adapted by the Hakka miners in West Borneo to serve as an instrument of political control throws open many questions and points to the need to examine other Chinese institutions which might have similarly evolved in Southeast Asia during the past two or three centuries.

At the same time, the *kongsi* as a distinctive Chinese response to the need for a kind of Civil Society for a Chinese community outside the country deserves further attention. The *kongsi* may not be simply an institution to protect production, marketing and entrepreneurship, but may also be an extension of inherent civic qualities in Chinese society which could not develop within the Confucian bureaucratic state but flourished when far away from literati supervision and from orthodox clan controls. It gives us a chance to ask whether the emergence of certain social tendencies and structures among the Chinese overseas in modern times are all due to their living among non-Chinese and learning foreign ways, or whether intrinsic Chinese norms among traders and landless workers are responsible for the way these external Chinese are adapting to the modern world.

Indeed we might go further to ask if some of these attitudes and structures have survived in China today. If they have, what changes have happened to them during the transition from a monarchy suffused by agrarian values to a revolutionary state determined to industrialize as quickly as possible? And now that romantic revolution has been replaced by practical reform, now that ideological control is feeble if any, could the native genius for social and economic organization be re-discovered and urged to generate a modern spirit of partnership and a new civic brotherhood?

We should not read too much into the fragmentary historical texts left behind by literati officials and their followers, but where Wang Tai Peng shows us reports by non-Chinese observers that corroborate and illuminate obscure Chinese relationships that officials have frowned upon or deliberately neglected, we do need to take heed. The author will be the first to admit that he has only begun to explore some of the intermediate relationships between people when they have to live, or settle, outside China. What he has done, however, is to show decisively how much Chinese people could do, when they were without state and family, to meet the challenges of a foreign and often hostile world.

Wang Gungwu
University of Hong Kong

Fig. 1. Front. } der Palissadering
Fig. 2. Profiel }

Fig. 1.   Fig. 2.

a. Ts-pekong.
bb Kamers voor den kapi-
   tein en de schrijvers.
cc Zalen voor algemeene
   bijeenkomsten.
dd Kamers voor vreemde gas-
   ten
ee Magazijnen.
ff Open plaatsen.
ğ Kookplaatsen.

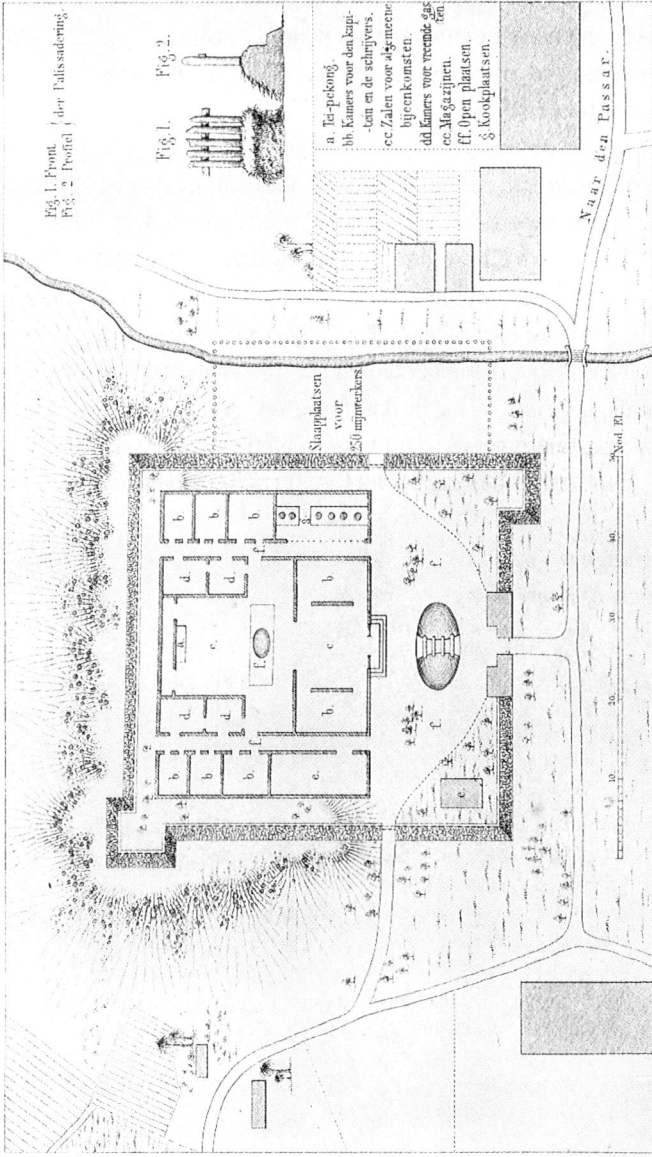

Slaapplaatsen
voor
250 mijnwerkers.

Naar den Passar.

KONINGS-HUIS TE MANDOR (1822)

INTRODUCTION

A precise definition and translation of the term *kongsi* is, as Schlegel has pointed out, almost impossible.[1] However, it is of necessity in this introduction of the book to set out various ways in which the term has been used and, in contrast to all of them, the particular sense that I will use.

Old and new usages of the word sprang to life all over the islands of Southeast Asia, with waves of Chinese immigration and the evolution of the Chinese ways of life that have become Chinese institutions such as the *kongsi*. Of all the general usages, the account given by *Beknopte Encyclopaedië van Nederlandsche Oost-Indië* is by far the best, the clearest and the most detailed:[2]

> *Kongsi* is a Chinese word which indicates a firm partnership or society in a very broad sense. The word has been commonly used in the archipelago over centuries and has become current in both Dutch and various native languages. Literally it means government by a general public or administration of public affairs. The word, *kongsi*, is derived from the dialect of the Hokkien people who have established themselves throughout Java and commercial ports of the outer islands. In the Hakka dialect, it reads as *kung-sze*. In Riouw and Java, administrators of a firm are customarily addressed and referred to as *kongsi*. Chinese officials also used this title.
>
> Owing to the untiring pursuit of the Chinese of the means to raise capital, the Chinese *kongsi* is numerous not only in our colony but also in the Malay Peninsula, in the outer islands of Indonesia and in the Philippines. The significance of the *kongsi* for the flowering

---

1. Gustaat Schlegel, *Tian ti Hwui* the Hung-league, or Heaven-earth league, Batavia, Haque, 1866, p.451.
2. T.J. Bezemer, *Beknopte Encyclopaedië van Nederlandsche Oost-Indië*, (Leiden, 1921) p.254.

1

and development of Chinese industry, commerce and navigation is hard to underestimate. The *kongsi* were entirely established to hold people of the same home countries and clans in a closer tie or relationship. In the family *kongsi*, no one, because of the tradition, could have private fortune so long as their father lived. All the family capital were at the disposal of the patriarch. Undoubtedly, if under closer examination, many *kongsi* would no longer be family *kongsi* as they at first seem to be. The Chinese *kongsi* have, however, become more and more divorced from the above-mentioned origins over time, more especially recently.

This is not all. In fact, almost every Chinese institution during the nineteenth century was called *kongsi*. A temple patron god, a clan society or a provincial club of the Chinese overseas was often named *kongsi* on foundation. Nevertheless, during the later part of the nineteenth century, they became better known as *hui-kuan*,[3] a name that was actually much older than *kongsi*, appearing in the sixteenth century.

Chinese 'secret' societies, however, were also-called *kongsi*. This had caused a great deal of confusion in the mind of the colonial authorities. The British administration in the Straits Settlements, for example, had been confusing *hui-kuan* with *hui* or 'secret' societies until 1892[4] when it began to draw a clear-cut line between them. But then this attempt to separate the goats from the sheep was only real from the point of view of the administration. As for the Chinese, as Purcell observes, no such distinction was made between good and bad.[5]

Hui or brotherhood is more proper a term to the vehicle of Chinese self-government as it was then the term *secret society*. The term 'secret

---

3. Ho Ping-ti has gone great lengths into the research of the evolution of *hui-kuan*, which he translates as hostels for examination candidates and goes only thus far. But already by the end of the Ming dynasty, something of modern unionism came of the *hui-kuan* movement of the Ssu-chou weavers. This, however, is not included in Ho's definition of *hui-kuan*. See Ho Ping-ti, *The Ladder of Success in Imperial China*, (New York, 1962) pp.208-9, and his *Chung-kuo Hui-kuan Shih-lun*.
4. S.S.S.B., 1892, 02,3.
5. Purcell, 1962 edition, p.272.

society' is all the more misleading for the objection raised by Purcell, whatever the precise implication of secrecy may have been:[6]

> All Chinese social organization was necessarily 'secret' whilst it was not recognized or was banned by the Government. The Chinese municipal organizations in Borneo, the *kongsis*, were, and are, referred to as 'secret societies', as are all Chinese political organization in Siam where they are illegal.

Modern scholarship has now widely recognized the so called 'secret' societies as the vehicles of the Chinese autonomy within the colonial rule in Southeast Asia.[7] But despite this recognition, the term 'secret society' remains.

Chinese *kongsi* that emerges in Southeast Asia in the eighteenth century, rooted as they were in both Chinese partnership and brotherhood traditions, were only new in the regions. Their origins, unlike the Chinese brotherhood in an attempt to overthrow the Ch'ing dynasty, were entirely related to the rise of overseas Chinese mining industries. But although some of the Chinese *kongsi* in Southeast Asia may have carried over the ritual oath-taking ceremony and even the name of T'ien-Ti Hui, they generally evolved from a small partnership, either in commerce or mining. On foundation, they were called *hui* or union, after which was commonly misused in early colonial days to mean a

6. Purcell, 1952 edition, p.328.
7. M.F. Somers Heidhues, *Southeast Asia's Chinese Minorities* (London, 1974) p.48.
8. W. Blythe, p.552. A perfect example of how a colonial writer would view a *hui* was Cameron who has said this: "Instead of forgetting their national prejudices, or postponing their indulgence of them till their return to China, the people of each province clan together and form a *hoey* or secret society. The avowed object of these *hoeys* is to afford mutual protection, but they are often used for the infliction of wrong, and have been found a great stumbling-block to the perfect administration of justice in the law courts of the Straits." See Cameron, *Our Tropical Possessions in Malayan India* (London, 1865) p.142.
9. The *Toa Peh Kong* in Penang, it seems, in the description of T.S. Lewis, was the brotherhood of merchants and traders who were closely connected in business transactions with Europeans, their friends and dependants. Lewis spoke of the T'ien-Ti Hui in Penang being the Ghee Hin, Hysan and Hoh Siang, who are all, it is said, under one and the same partnership although acting separate bodies. See K.K. Khoo, *The Western Malay States 1850-1874*, (London, 1972) p.113.

'secret' society.[8] Later, when they grew into large organizations with hundreds or thousands of members, they were known as *kongsi*. The T'ien-Ti Hui in Penang was a partnership in origin.[9] Much of the same thing, however, can be said of the early Chinese community in the Straits Settlements and Malay States, which was made up of a number of *hui* or *kongsi*. [10]

Recent writers have offered a variety of definitions of *kongsi*. *Kongsi* is understood by Blythe as any partnership or group with a common interest.[11] Barbara Ward defines it as 'the large political groups in the mining districts', which seems rather vague. J.C. Jackson is much more specific. He only uses the term *kongsi* to signify alliances of mining unions and their farming and mining members.[12] I myself define it neither simply as partnership or brotherhood, nor a combination of both. Rather, my definition of *kongsi* is that it was a form of open government, based on an enlarged partnership and brotherhood. Its purpose was to protect economic gains as well as to resist outside powers. In this form of government, every member had equal rights in the process of government as everyone was an equal partner and brother to the other. The administration is open to public criticism, participation, election, or dismissal by a general meeting in the *kongsi-*house. This new political organization provided a foundation for the social and economic life of the overseas Chinese.

The newness of *kongsi* government, particularly its representative function, public accessibility, and direct democracy, did not go unnoticed by Western observers in the early nineteenth century, and by the Chinese a century later. The Westerners who saw *kongsi* through the distorting lens of western concepts found it to be something of a

---

10. Chen Yü-shung has clearly understood that clans or *Pan* formed by secret societies provided the foundation of early Singapore's Chinese community. Many Chinese temples were during that time only the smoke screens of private associations or *hui* or brotherhoods and controlled by members of brotherhoods. Even those non-*hui* temples were also infiltrated by brotherhoods' members so much so that they were not unlike *hui* temples. See Lin Hsiao Sheng, *Ssu-la Ku-Chi,* p.1.

11. W. Blythe, p.553.

12. B.E. Ward, 'A Hakka Kongsi of Borneo', *Journal of Oriental Studies*, Vol.1, p.359, n.12.

republic. Similarly those Chinese scholars using the same lens, have also found republic elements in *kongsi*. Such an approach to the history of *kongsi* is evidently Eurocentric. *Kongsi*, no doubt, bear some resemblance to western democracy and republicanism, but this resemblance lies only in government by elected representatives. Beyond that, an equation of *kongsi* government with western democracy would be completely misleading. *Kongsi* government was essentially a synthesis of extended partnership and sworn-brotherhood, which was uniquely Chinese. No western democracy, however open and direct, was or is such a system.[13] Nevertheless my study does not pretend to present a Chinese point of view from inside. Though as far as possible, I have tried to enter the minds of the Chinese of the *kongsi* in the West Borneo, my vision remains that of an outsider who looks at it from a great distance of time.

Kongsi government is here presented as genuine Chinese 'democracy' without western influence. This approach derived from a consideration of its roots, which were deeply buried in the Chinese past. Its origins – the Chinese partnership system – had grown into maturity as early as the twelfth century when the *huo-chi* system gave rise to a managerial class. By that time, the system had already spread from the mountains in China to the seas to Japan and to Southeast Asia. Throughout the Sung dynasty, the Chinese partnership systems, though important economically, had no major political system. During the Ming dynasty, however, Chinese partnership systems grew much more complex and became the foundation of Chinese economic life. Particularly two social groups, who were most adventurous and freedom loving, the sea-merchants and illegal miners, began during that period to construct their own government on the basis of partner-

---

13. Bertrand Russell has mentioned a 34-year old experiment of partnership for all by J.S. Lewis who made all the workers in his enterprises partners who share in profit and share actively in the government of the whole enterprises. This as well as the move towards Industrial Democracy in the present day is something along the same line as the Chinese *kongsi* perhaps. But industrial democracy goes only as far as the regulation of industry and not the whole process of government, which was open to all members in Chinese *kongsi*. Bertrand Russell, *Authority and the Individual*, (London, 1974) p.76.

ship systems. In building their democratic self-government, they combined the partnership systems with brotherhood. Consequently, ever since 1455, when the rebellion of Teng Mao-Chi pioneered a new way of life based on the equality of partnership, illegal miners rose up incessantly to fight for their brotherhood government. There were also brotherhood government of sea-merchants who were called 'pirates' in ·official history. Such sea-merchant kingdoms in which the king was the leader of the whole brotherhood and partnership, provided another kind of political partnership.

It is clear that the Chinese people had begun to think in earnest about the possibility of brotherhood government as a political alternative. After the fall of the Ming dynasty, what the Chinese people was actually trying to do was not to put the clock back. Instead, they attempted to institute a new form of government, the brotherhood government. This was the basic purpose of nation-wide rising of the T'ien-Ti Hui and of the Taiping Revolution. Unfortunately, the T'ien-Ti Hui has all too often been misinterpreted as a restorationist cause and a secret society movement, and the Taiping Revolution as only another peasant uprising. This obscures the fundamental shift of Chinese political thinking towards Liberalism since the late Ming. It is, however, saddening to observe that the Chinese people did not succeed in establishing a lasting brotherhood government to replace Chinese monarchy in China. Among a great variety of complex reasons, the chief one, I think, is that they tried to fuse their brotherhood government with the old political framework – Chinese monarchy. *Kongsi* government, typified by those in West Borneo, was, on the contrary, completely free from such conservatism. Equality of partnership in it found full expression in direct 'democracy' and the open process of government. This very special kind of brotherhood government was undreamt of in China, and perhaps, elsewhere in the world as well. The seeds of it lay in China, but it only bore fruits in West Borneo, then throughout Southeast Asia.

By the end of the nineteenth century, the tradition of Chinese *kongsi* or Chinese self-government had been uprooted by the determined effort of the western powers who came to dominate Southeast Asia. The term *kongsi* survived the western impact, but its original political function as Chinese self-government had been so diminished it now meant no more than a commercial company. Once the *kongsi* was reduced to shadow of its former self, the great significance of its emergence throughout Southeast Asia in the eighteenth and nineteenth centuries seem to have been forgotten, even among historians. Some of them still cling to the image of *kongsi* as a secret society, whether criminal or legitimate. Others, notably those who use the distorting lens of western concepts, call them republics. These misunderstandings lead to a static, undynamic picture not only of *kongsi* but also of much of Chinese history. To date, scholarship has suggested that the Chinese people never created any form of democracy, never experienced democracy or democratic life as part of their historical traditions. The general picture is still a very conservative one, in which western contact or impact alone have revolutionized Chinese values and society as a whole. The demolition of such conscious or unconscious conservatism in the understanding of Chinese history can only be done by collective efforts and to this end I contribute my own part. This study is not an attempt to revive the glory of the Chinese *kongsi*, nor to recover a paradise lost. It is simply a reconstruction of the Chinese past connected with *kongsi* in a way that, by differing sharply from the standard views, instils a far greater sense of dynamism into history, and into our past, present, and future.

Chapter 1

KONGSI ROOTS IN THE ORGANIZATIONAL FRAMEWORK ITSELF AND YÜNNAN

1. Background to the Origins of the *Kongsi*.

De Groot's theory that the village institution in China held the origins of the Chinese *kongsi* still goes unchallenged as the standard view. J.C. Jackson, Barbara E. Ward and Tien alike inherited this view. Even De Groot's most severe critic, Schaannk, never challenged this theory.

According to it, the autonomous Chinese village institution embodies the western principle of democracy by a general election of the village head.[1] It also argues that most of the Chinese in the west Borneo came from the countryside of China, and only an insignificant number of them were from the cities.[2] After their arrival, clan and family ties formed the basic of unity. They elected a head or patriarch who served as a rallying point in safeguarding their well-being. The Chinese village institution was thus replanted in a foreign land.[3] This theory goes hand in hand with a traditional view that the Chinese peasants were driven overseas by wars, poverty, natural disasters and varying forms of exploitation.

Another widely accepted interpretation is the secret society theory which is more sophisticated and divergent. Wen Hsiung-fei and Wang Chia-chien regard the kongsi as the overseas branches of the T'ien-Ti Hui.[4] Veth agrees with them in part, but he places more emphasis on the local relevance of the *kongsi*.[5] To Schaannk, the *kongsi* were not a proliferation of the T'ien-ti Hui at all. They were secret societies en-

---

1. J.J. De Groot, *Het Kongsiwezen van Borneo* (Leiden 1895) pp.84,85.
2. Ibid., p.117.
3. Ibid.
4. Wang Chia-chien, 'Wei Yüan, his concept on the Maritime Defence and his understanding of the West', (Taipei, 1964) p.37.
5. P.J. Veth, *Borneo's Wester-afdeeling* (leiden, 1856) Vol.1, p.311.

.tirely founded for local aims. Local aims were of particular importance to the formation of the *kongsi*. For instance, long before 1854, secret societies of Montrado's *kongsi* were formed with an aim to overthrow the Ta-kang *kongsi*.[6] In addition, within the *kongsi* themselves, the half-caste Chinese organized their own brotherhood against the pure Chinese.[7]

Instead of plunging into a debate with all these prevailing views, I would rather first try to find out what the *kongsi* were about and how they were formed.

Chinese sources in regards to the *kongsi* organization are woefully sketchy. Still, they are indispensable.

1. *Wan-kuo ti-li t'u-chih.*[8]

   "The Chia-yinese went into the mountains to open up the gold mines. They themselves established a country and selected the elders called *kongsi* to run the administration for a period of one or two years."

2. *Mei-yüeh tung-chi chuan.*[9]

   "Tens of thousands of Cantonese had come to Larat opening up the gold mines and washing the gold-dust. For fear of the fierce barbarians, they established their own heads in the same way as the local chiefs ruled their subjects."

3. *Ying-huan chih-lueh.*[10]

   "... They elected the elders to be the k'o-chang who administered the *kongsi* for one or two years."

These sources only tell us that much. The chronicles of Lan-fang *kongsi* adds little more to them:[11]

1. *Ta-ko*, headman or eldest brother.
2. *Fu-t'ou-jen*, assistant headman.
3. *Wei-ko lao-ta*, assistant headman, elder brother.

---

6. Schaannk, "De Kongsi's van Montrado" in *TITLV*, Vol.xxxv, Nos.5 & 6, p.587.
7. Schaannk, p.487.
8. Wei Yuan, *Hai-kuo t'u-chih* (An illustrated treatise on the maritime kingdoms) chuan 12, Hai-tao-kuo 2, p.1 orig. pub. 1841
9. Ibid., p.3.
10. Ibid., p.5.
11. Appendix in Lo., p.141.

Ta-ko presided over the whole kongsi as the head of state. *Fu-t'ou-jen* and *wei-ko lao-ta* were elected to both the district and central positions of leadership. But, while *fu-t'ou-jen* was paid by the *kongsi*, *wei-ko lao-ta* only held an honorary position.

Unlike the Chinese sources in China, the English sources provide first-hand information. Earl, who had personally visited Montrado, called the leaders *kongsi* and the ordinary gold miners 'coolies'.[12]

In Takang *kongsi*, each district, according to him, was governed by several representatives who were called *kongsi*. They, in turn, elected the governor to the central leadership. Important matters were not left to the governor alone. He was expected to consult the district representatives.[13]

Although Crawfurd himself had not been in Montrado, he was informed by the Chinese that there were 13 large gold mines and 57 small ones. The large gold mines were in general operated under the wage system. Monthly wages were given to the workers by the capitalists. In contrast, the small mines were operated under the *kongsi* system. The labourers conducted the operation and shared the proceeds on terms of perfect equality.[14] Generally, the large mines employed 100 to 200 men, including both labourers and overseers. The work force of small mines was 10 to 50.[15]

Finally, Dutch sources: they are the best informed for the obvious reason that they were derived from a long and direct contact with the *kongsi*. Therefore, we are able to draw some diagrams of the organization based on them:

| District *kongsi* | 2 or more clerks *(Djoeroe-toelis)* in charge of finance, daily administration and police. |
| | 1 or more overseer *(ma'lim)* who supervised the miners at work and collected the gold from them. (4 months' office) |

---

12. G.W. Earl, *The Eastern Seas* (London, 1837) p.279.
13. Earl, pp.290,291.
14. J. Crawfurd, *History of the Indian Archipelago*, (London, 1820) Vol.iii, pp.474,475.
15. Ibid.

Central *kongsi*	1 general head (*kapitan* or *panglima*) 2 clerks, one for finance administration, the other for provision. 1 *ma'lim* keeping money and accounts 7 *ts'ai-k'u* or *orang tuah*, representatives from the subordinate *kongsi*

Source: Veth, Vol.1, pp.319,320.

Officer of 4 months office	1 *huo-chang* or inspector, who ruled the labourers, saw to the steady progress of work, regulated work hours and settled disputes in the mines and taking care of the waterwork.
Officers of 4 months office	2 *Djoeroe-toelis* or administrators who kept accounts, purchased all the necessities, dealt with correspondence and legal proceedings. 3 *ts'ai-k'u mandoor*s or foreman. They were the heads of lower rank.

Source: De Rees: Montrado p.28

Great mines	2 *huo-chang* mine heads 3 *ts'ai-k'u* including 1 book-keeper, 1 money keeper and 1 storekeeper 8 *ting-kung* foreman
Small mines	1 *huo-chang* 2 *ts'ai-k'u* 3 *ting-kung*

Source: Schaannk, p.571

From all the above sources, we may put a whole picture of *kongsi* organization together in a list. It will enable us to see very clearly that many different terms and titles were used by those holding the same position in the administration.

POSITION	TITLES	SOURCES
1. The highest leader	*Kapitan* *ta-ko* *Po*	Veth Yeh Hsian-yün Yeh, Schaannk
2. Head	*kongsi* *tung-shih* *k'o-chang* *fu-t'ou-jen* *huo-chang*	Wan-kuo ti-li Earl Yeh Hsi Chi-yu Hsien Ch'ing-kao Yeh ˙ De Rees Schaannk
3. Clerk	*Djoeroe-toelis* *ts'ai-ku*	Veth, De Rees Schaannk
4. Foreman	*ma'lim* *ts'ai-k'u* *ting-kung*	Veth De Rees Schaannk
5. Ordinary worker	*coolie* *kung-jen* *huo-chi*	Earl Yeh Schaannk

The term *kung-jen* is used by Yeh when he related the episode of Lo's conquest of the gold lake.[16] The workers under *tung-shih* Chang A-chai were won over by Lo and treated as his brothers.[17] Such brotherly treatment was not a strategy nor limited to Lan-fang *kongsi*. Brotherhood was a tradition of *kongsi*. It was a way of life in the pioneering *kongsi* which could not survive otherwise.

Ts'ai-k'u was not a foreman. Obviously, De Rees has made a mistake here, because the term itself in Chinese means treasurer.

There seems to have been two modes of production in Montrado. In the big mines, the division between capital and labour was distinctive.

The small mines, however, seem as yet to show no evidence of class polarization. In the Chinese tin mining *kongsi* of Banka in the early eighteen century, fraternity and equality were a living reality. In the words of Thomas Horsefield:

---

16. Appendix in Lo, p.138
17. Ibid.

13

No difference of rank or conditions amongst the workmen at one mine; the work is undertaken in fellowship and they share equally in the produce; the labour connected with the process of mining is performed by all indiscriminately.[18]

Nevertheless, in West Borneo, it was equally true of the small or pioneering *kongsi*. There, those who worked at a daily rate were called *kuli-kongsi*. Of course, they were the wage labourers in a modern sense. On the other hand, those workers who participated in the gain or loss were called *hun* (hokkien dialect) or *fen*.[19]

All the terms which we have pieced together are very significant. In fact, they are the living organism in the body of *kongsi*. Each term represents an origin or history of a system. Each system is closely linked with the rise of Chinese private enterprise, which was already afoot as early as the twelfth century.

2. Links with Yünnan's Private Copper Mining
– *K'o-chang*, *Mi-fen* and *Coolie*

The *fen* system

When and where were the *k'o-chang*, *coolie* and *fen* systems born? Before they had found their ways overseas, what were they all then? Certainly they were not the sea birds that could themselves migrate overseas. Their migration instead was done by the bearers of the systems – the miners. What were these people then? Were they originally peasants? Merchants? Or miners? Were they from the countryside or the cities of China? Whatever they were, one thing is sure, they were the people who had learnt at least something about mining technology and organization in China.

In the Yünnan copper mining which began to be of national significance about 1685,[20] all these systems could be found. But the *fen* system itself seems to have already been operative in organizing cop-

---

18. Thomas Horsfield, 'Sketch of the Process of Mining' in *Journ. of Ind. Arch.*, 1848, Vol.2, p.811.
19. Posewitz, *Borneo: Its Geology and Mineral Resources* (London, 1892) p.359.
20. Yen Chung-p'ing, *Ch'ing-tai Yun-nan tung-cheng-kao*, (Shanghai, 1948) p.1.

per mining in Yünnan two centuries earlier. Wang Shih-hsin testifies as follows:[21]

> Everywhere Yunnan is rich with mine ore. Where the mines are yet to be established, the small people go to dig the ore freely. They only make a bare subsistence for themselves. But once the mines are already established the mine-heads or *tung-t'ou* report them to the official to apply for licences. Depending on the size of the mine, the mine-head decides how many miners or *i-fu* to be recruited. All of them are under his control.
>
> Before the mine has got going, every expense is borne by the mine-head himself. For a big mine, the expenses amounted to thousands of taels. When the ore is already dug out and ready for processing, the official inspects it. Everyday, the miners go into the mine to work. In the evening, they bring the ore out and pile it into heaps which they divide into four. One heap goes to the official tax, one to the common expenses, one to the mine-head, and one heap is divided again by the miners themselves on an equal basis.

This was legal mining. Meanwhile, the official records were crowded with a lot of illegal mining activities. Some illegal mining were carried on secretly and quietly in the remote mountains beyond the reach of the official. But a number of them took the form of armed resistance, openly challenging the authorities. From 1442, the official monopoly policy on silver mining touched off incessant miner uprisings which ended only about 1639, with the Ming dynasty.[22]

The uprising of Yeh Chung-liu in 1455 was inaugurated with a note of warning which the miners sent to the Ming official:

> You better let us have the silver mine or *ch'ang* at Pao-feng (in the border area of Fukien and Chekiang), otherwise, we will kill you.[23]

And so they openly seized the official silver mines one after another by force, flouting the authorities. The actual uprising itself was

---

21. Wang Shih-hsin, *Kuan-chin-i-i* v.5 in Lee Lung-chien, 'A tentative view on the elements of capitalism in the Ming mining industry', in *CKTP* Vol.2, p.230.
22. Pai Shou-i, 'The development of the mining industry in the Ming period' in *CKTP*, pp.964, 965.
23. *Ming Ying-chung Shih-lu*, 136;1.

sparked off by an attempt of a Ming official, Chu-yen, to arrest the miners. Chu-yen was killed by them and Yeh proclaimed himself a king.[24] Yeh's forces are said to have been only a few hundred, although it seems more probably to have been 2000 at least.[25] However, their ranks were soon swelled with followers who were given the confiscated property of corrupt officials and landlords. As a result, county after county fell into their hands, and the whole border area between Fukien and Chekiang was controlled by them.

A revolution blazed away in 1448 when they allied themselves with the more powerful insurgent groups comprising merchants, miners, poor citizens, and peasants led by Teng Mao-chi. Teng Mao-chi, who is said to have been an illegal miner himself, fled to Lin-hua of Fukien and established himself as a leader of the merchant union there.[26] As a way to publicize his revolutionary manifesto, he proclaimed himself the King of Equality and vowed in public to demolish every inequality in the imperial rule.[27] Within a year their forces had snowballed into hundreds of thousand, and they had complete control over the whole of Fukien province. Although the regime of miners and merchants was very short-lived, it did, in that period, mark a turning point. The potential for social change had already begun to emerge in Chinese history.

---

24. *Ming-shih*, 172;60;12, 'History of Ming'.
25. *Ming-shih chi-shih Pen-mo*, 31;1, *Hung Chiu-lu*, 10;121. Lee Lung-chien, 'The characteristics of the uprising of Yeh Chung-liu and Teng Mao-chi', in *Li-shih chiao-hsueh*, (Peking, 1957) No.3, p.12.
26. Lee Lung-chien, p.16.
   Hung chiu-lu, 9;119, 10;121.
   Teng's rise to influence in the local community derived much from his command of two very important office. His presidency of a village market which he had personally founded gathered increasing number of followers among the merchants, peasants and peddlers. His office of the *Tsung-hsiao-chia* (the superintendent of village guards) enabled him to command the local defence forces for his armed backing. The positions were indeed the ladder to success for the men with no particular social status nor great means and wealth like him.
   M. Tanaka, in *Mindaishi Ronso* (Tokyo, 1962) p.642.
27. *Fu-chien t'ung-chih*, (Provincial gazetteer of Fukien) Comp. by Ch'en Shou-sh'i, 1968. 8:5.

Illegal mining promised no success, no security, no comfort. Nonetheless, to the miners it offers something like a paradise. Private mining, both legal and illegal, was all based on the *fen* system.[28] But in illegal mining the profit was shared only among the miners, including the leader, and official tax was out of the question. It offered freedom from the official exploitation, the equality of profit-sharing, and the brotherhood in which they lived.

The *fen* system in the early Ch'ing period had ultimately grown into a synthesis of the *coolie* and *huo-chi* systems. It was this synthesis which contributed considerably to the Yünnan copper boom so well known in Chinese mining history. Wang Shung relates how in general the copper mining started in great detail:[29]

> As a rule, the mining settlements or *ch'angs* are situated in remotest mountains...The miners or *ch'ang-min* opened the copperfields by digging tunnels through the mountains...The leader who supplied capital and recruited workers was called *kuan-shih*. Everyone in the settlement regardless of status is called *ti-hsiung*, brother, or *hsiao-huo-chi*, small partner.

Much overlapping of terms often occurred within the same system. *Kuan-shih* was also called *huo-fang* by Tang Chui and *wo-t'ou* by Ni Chen-sheu. *Ch'ang* in the pioneering period was called *huo-fang*, which was established by twenty or thirty people who brought some provisions and built tents there. Oil and rice were the most important things to them, oil for burning lamps in mines, rice for meals.[30] As for establishing a *huo-fang*, as Yen suggests, it required only a small amount of capital.[31] Since the headman who pioneered the *huo-fang* had the job of raising capital, it was not surprising that he was called *huo-fang* or *wo t'ou*.

---

28. Pai had mistaken Yeh Chung-liu as the employer of the miners whom he led in seizing government mines. Yeh was, I believe, actually a *tung-tou* or a leader of the miners who raised the common fund. cf. Pai, pp.985,986.
29. Wang Shung, 'Kuan-ch'ang chai-len pen' in *YTCK* Vol.9, Chap.73, p.14.
30. Wang Shung, p.65.
31. Yen Chung-p'ing, p.67.

17

The *fen* system to which the origin of the Chinese *kongsi* in Southeast Asia is referred, was a way to share capital and profit. Originally, it was called *mi-fen*. This could be a group of people who gathered together to launch a mining enterprise. Mostly, they were friends or relations of each other. Each of them went around to borrow rice and pooled their resources together. The profits were divided by each one in accordance with how much rice he had contributed to the common fund.[32]

Mi-fen could also be one such case described by Ni Lui as follows:[33]

> The news of the discovery of a new mine-field brought people with capital from far and near to Yünnan. These people are called *ch'ang-ko*. Sometimes, one person alone and sometimes a few people together choose a mine, estimate the needed number of miners and the cost of daily necessities. Then, accordingly the fund or capital is raised. When the mine makes a profit, it is split into ten shares after tax. One goes to the technician and foreman, three to the workers, and six to the *ch'ang-ko*.

The *coolie* system

The original meaning of the term *coolie* is quite the opposite of the present usage. Far from being a derogatory term for the unskilled worker or porter, it was a term that gave everyone involved in the mining partnership an equal status. It was all embracing, as Wu Chi-chuan stated:[34]

> Gathering partners to open up a mine together is called *shih-fen*. *Shih-fen* is actually *mi-fen*. The *coolie* call the *tung-fu* (the one who raises capital) *wo-t'ou*. The *tung-fu* calls the *coolies ti-hsiung*. The titles of *coolies* differ widely according to the jobs and responsibilities.

Coolie here meant hired labour and *tung-fu* the people of the mine. The reason why the one who founded the mine was called *wo-t'ou* is

32. Yuan Yuan, comp. *Yünnan t'ung-chih-kao* (a General Gazetteer of Yunnan), (1835), hereafter *YNTCK*, Vol.9, chuan. 74. Kuan-ch'ang 2. p.22.
33. Ni Lui, 'A letter in discussion of the matters of mining settlements' in *Huang-ch'ao chih-shih wen-pien*, (1873) chuan 52, ch'ang-chi, p.14.
34. Wu Chi-chun, in Peng, ed. *SKYSCL* (1840-1849) Vol.1 (Peking 1967) p.338.

already explained above. But it is significant that the *tung-fu* called all his *coolies* brothers and they called him *wo-t'ou*. *Coolies* included the manager, *kuan-shih*, the instructor, *hsiang-t'ou*, the overseer, *hin-pan*, the profit-sharing worker, *ch'in-sheng* and the monthly wage worker, *yueh-huo* and so on.[35] The term *coolie* embraced a wide spectrum of workers, skilled and unskilled, employed on a basis of wage or partnership.

The *mi-fen* system combined the *coolie* and *huo-chi* systems together. Thus, everyone in the mine was called *ti-hsiung*, brother or *hsiao-huo-chi*, small partner. This is a fact I have already mentioned, a fact that speaks for itself. Although *coolie* was apparently never used by the employer, *ch'ang-ko*, but only by the employees in calling themselves, both the *ch'ang-ko* and his *coolie* were partners to each other. They were equal to each other socially, although *ch'ang-ko* had a bigger share in the profit. The brother in the mine was actually based on the *mi-fen* system which bound the *ch'ang-ko* and *coolie* together.

The *k'o-chang* system

K'o-chang played a pivotal role in those self-ruled mining settlements. As T'an-Ts'ui related:[36]

> In every mining settlement, the people elect an honest and experienced person as their head. He is called *k'o-chang*. With the consensus of the people, he sets up the severest rules. Anyone who offends the rules, takes the punishment and humiliation without complaint.

He acted as the arbitrator to settle disputes over mining rights as well.[37] With such a power and prestige invested in him, he embodied the self-government of the mines. His power to enforce the law and order set up by the miners themselves was identical to that of the leaders of the *kongsi* in West Borneo. But, his power was reduced to the shadow of its former self, when the government exerted its control

35. Ibid.
36. T'an Ts'ui, p.3.
37. Wang Shung, p.15.

over mines. In cases like big mining settlements too big to avoid official control or big mines financed by big capital, an official was appointed by the government to rule the settlement.[38] This official was called *ch'ang chu* responsible for jurisdiction and taxation. *K'o-chang* was but one of the seven heads who served as the administrators under him. The power of *k'o-chang* was reduced to controlling the merchants in the mining town. Consequently, the autonomy of the mining settlement had lost in eclipse of *k'o-chang*.

Small mines in the remote mountains were outside the government's control. In order to remain independent, they used the tactics of guerrilla warfare against the Ch'ing government. Some of them like *Ch'ing-lung-shan* (Green Dragon Mountain) and *Funghuan-p'o* (Phoenix Slope) were situated in deep and remote mountains. Some of them like *Chien-chu* (arrow-bamboo) and *Chin-sha* (Golden-sand) mines were joined with the border of neighbouring provinces. The tracks there were spreading like the veins of leaves to everywhere. The illegal miners always hid there to dig the mines or process the copper. They had chosen the high mountains or deep forests for escape. Once, the government troops attempted to track them down, but they all disappeared quickly without a trace.[39] Wang Tai-yüeh, a Ch'ing official, thus described them as cunning and stubborn without any official identification of their own origins. To them, there was no way that the Ch'ing government was going to successfully exert its control.

They, nevertheless, did not refuse to pay tax. What they resisted was the official control. Out of a tank of copper, 20 to 30 catties went to the government, and a few catties to the *k'o-chang* and his *hsi-t'ou*, the leader of the metal workers. The rest of it was shared by the miners who brought it to trade in elsewhere far away.[40] The number of the autonomous mines is said to have amounted to twenty or thirty.[41]

---

38. Ibid. On the administration of mines, see also Yen Chung-p'ing
39. Wang Tai-yueh, in *HCCS*, 52;8.
40. Ibid.
41. Ibid.

In fact, the so called 'small' mines were not small at all. When the copper boom was at its beginning, the big mines are said to have employed tens of thousands of people and even in the small ones the miners were counted by the thousands.[42] The workers in both big and small mines increased tenfold in the full bloom of the copper boom.[43] The big mine was counted by hundreds of thousands of people and the ·small mine by tens of thousands. A mine which employed thousands to tens of thousands of people is not small by any standards especially if compared with those Chinese mining settlements in Southeast Asia.

Soon, the copper boom attracted big capital from everywhere. Big merchant groups from Hunnan, Hupei, Kiansu, Kiangsi, Chekiang, Szechuan, Kwangtung and Kwanghsi provinces poured in their investments. To open a mine, they usually spent 100,000 to 200,000 taels.[44]

Meanwhile, labourers from all these provinces were also attracted by the booming industry in Yünnan. As a result of the influx of these people, the total number of the miners amounted to more than a million.[45] During the hey day of the boom (1736-1821), there was said to have been well over 300 mines in Yünnan. Though the small miners were far more numerous, their production in total was less than half that of the big mines.[46]

In general, the economic foundation of the big mines was the monthly wage system, and as a rule, they were directly controlled by the government. The small mines by contrast, still retained the *mi-fen* system and their autonomy.

---

42. Ni Sheng-shu in *YTCK*, 74; *Kuan-ch'ang* 2:26
     The Ch'ing court set a price to buy copper from the 20 over small mines around the Green Dragon Mountain. The price was that 4 taels for a hundred catties of copper. Whereas in other provinces, the price for a hundred catties of copper was 9 or 10 taels or even more. On the other hand, the Ch'ing official gave the big mines a much better price, 6.4 taels per hundred catties. Such a discrimination surely further fueled the resentment of the small mines. No wonder, the small mines fought desperately to withhold their autonomy and to smuggle out their copper.
     cf. Wang Tai-yüeh in *HCCS*, 52;6,7,8.
43. Peng, ed. *SKYS* (1840-1949) (Peking, 1957) p.339.
44. Ibid.
45. Ibid.
46. Wang Tai-yüeh, p.8.

In respect of the self-rule, the small mines in Yünnan had foreshadowed the Chinese *kongsi* overseas. The synthesis of the *mi-fen* and *coolie* systems had found a new form of existence in these *kongsi*. The Chinese miners in early Ming had built a democratic life on the basis of brotherhood and partnership in their mines. Already in 1448, a new social force headed by Teng Mao-chi pioneered a new way of life based on equality, on a new social values. Although the miner uprisings ended with the Ming dynasty, the incessant struggle for democracy and equality of the miners went on quietly in the illegal mining activities during the period of Ch'ing. The feudal regimes were only able to put down miners uprisings. But, they could never suppress the root of democracy and equality in the mines – the *fen* system that had gone deep into every single aspect of the Chinese private enterprise, alongside with the wage system.[47]

47. So far, no Chinese Marxist historians have had any good words for the *k'o-chang* system. All see it as an instrument of the feudal regime to oppress and exploit the miners. They are too biased to see that the root of autonomy in small mines lay in the system, to appreciate its revolutionary significance.

Li Shu, in *CKCS*, Vol.4, p.6.

Liu Yung-ch'eng, in *CKCS*, Vol.2, p.318.

Wang Ming-lun, in *CKCS* Vol.2, p.197.

He accuses the *mi-fen* system for exploiting the miners more than the wage system.

Ch'ung Han-hsian in *CKCS*, Vol.4, p.53.

Chapter 2

A HERITAGE FROM THE CHINESE PARTNERSHIP SYSTEMS IN THE LAND AND SEA

1. Equality of Partnership in the Land – the *Huo-chi* System

We have derived, from Yünnan mining *ch'ang*s, the answer to where the *k'o-chang* (head of a mining settlement), *coolie* and *mi-fen* (mining partnership) systems first arose. They seemed, however, to have left no trace as regards the origins of the *huo-chang* and *ts'ai-k'u* (treasurer) systems. Where were the origins of the systems? And is there any connection of significance between the origins of the two systems which seemed so disjointed and developed separately?

I think, there is. The indirect but essential 'blood-tie' is the *huo-chi* system. As mentioned above, in the *coolie* system. As mentioned above, in the *coolie* system, everyone was called *ti-hsiung* (brother) or *hsiao-huo-chi* (small partner). This fact forges a link between the *huo-chi* (partner) and *coolie* systems. The link, in fact, is not only in terminology. Both had so much in common in the most fundamental aspect – the sharing of capital and profits – and in the sense of partnership as well. Though I am not very sure as to which system derived from which, I have more evidence to show that the *huo-chi* system came earlier. The term *huo-chi* may have only come to light in late Ming, but the system itself went back as early as the Tang Dynasty. The system had already become widely used by different social groups during the Sung times. We are told that not only the sea-merchants, especially those from Fukien, the illegal tea merchants and salt merchants, but also the wine shopkeepers and the farmers used the system to get their business going.

By the time of Ming, the system grew dominant. It has spilled over to almost every aspect of Chinese economic life ever since. It had been recognized as the key to Shansi merchants' success in commerce by both *Chin-lu* and *Shao-i-chih*:

> The big merchants of *Ping-yang* and *ch'ih-lu* were the richest in China. Unless their wealth well passed the mark of hundreds of thousands taels, they would not regard themselves as rich. In doing business, they had an excellent way. Their method valued personal integrity above everything else. Everyone of those who worked together on a basis of partnership was called *huo-chi*. One of them supplied the capital and the rest shared it. Though no oath was taken, none of them would cheat each other. If someone had borrowed money with interest and died, even long after his death, his children or grandchildren would never fail to repay it. This unfailing repayment of debt was done even when it involved much sweat and toil. Therefore, other people with capital all scrambled to have them as commercial partners. The reason was that if they could honour the debt of the dead, certainly they would not betray the living. Once in a partnership, by paying only a little interest first, they could later have great profits fall into their laps. With or without capital, everyone of them was thereby able to have a means of livelihood. The rich, furthermore, did not keep their wealth idle at home, but instead dispersed it among commercial partners or *huo-chis*. Only the number of big or small commercial partnerships he had was thus counted when assessing an individual's wealth. In this way, many millionaires could be counted. Thanks to partnerships, the rich could not suddenly plummet into poverty, whereas the poor could shoot up to wealth immediately. Their commercial practice was so excellent and their personal integrity noble indeed.[1]

Shao-i-chih has also told another success story of the big merchants of *Shin-tu* whose riches had reached the standard of hundreds of thousands of taels. Their success was by no means a single man's effort. Very often, the big merchant had some assistants whose honesty in money won his complete trust. When the day of distributing the inter-

---

1. Fu I-ling, *Ming-ch'ing shih-tai shang-jen chi shang-yeh tzu-pen* (Merchants and Mercantile Capital in Ming and Ch'ing times), (Peking, 1956) p.86.
2. Hsi Ta-lin in *CKTP*, p.912.

est and profits came, the assistants then began to start their own business.[2]

·While it is difficult to determine in what province the system was popular in the twelfth century, we can pinpoint those in the Ming period with confidence. The *huo-chi* system was current among the merchant groups of Fukien, Kwantung, Kiansu and Chekiang, although Fu I-ling has only pointed out those of Shansi and Anhui.[3]

Throughout the sixteenth and seventeenth centuries, the *huo-chi* system rose to a new peak of strength with the significant growth of private enterprises not only in commerce but also in mining. A good example of its expansion was the private coal mining at Hsi-shan Ment-tou-kou in Peking, which started in 1596. As a result of angry demonstrations by investors, workers and porters against the official extortion, the Ming court had in 1603 adopted more liberal policy towards private coal mining.[4] However, what contributed most to a rapid growth of private coal mining after that, was not only these official concessions; it also flourished on the strength of the *huo-chi* system which gave it the framework of life. A contract of 1655 throws some light on the way the system worked:

> Entering upon a new partnership with Kao I and Yang Wen-hua, the contractor, Chiao Yün-lu was prepared to write off all the past expenses. Chiao is the landlord of the coal-mine as his grandfather had been, in the Ming dynasty, a partner of Kao's grandfather in coal mining. Now, in Ch'ing's time, Kao and Yang renewed the partnership by supplying the capital. It was agreed that the proceeds should be split into 60 *jih*s or divisions. Chiao is entitled to 10 *jih*s, Yang and Kao 30, and the Ching government 20. It was also agreed that profit-sharing would be on a basis of equality when the coal is produced and the cost of production deducted.[5]

> Nov. 11 the second year of the Shun Chih

---

3. The *huo-chi* system was widely practised in the Chinese junk trade notably carried by the sea-merchant groups of Fukien and Kwangtung. It will be dealt with in detail presently.

4. Teng Tuo, "From Wan Li to Ch'ien-lung" in *CKCS*, Vol.1, p.255.

5. Ibid., p.258.

Signatories of the partners *Witness*
    Yang Wen-hua   Sun Chien
    Kao I   Liu Ch'en-fang
    Chiao Yün-lu   Ch'ao Yin-feng

It is one out of the 137 contracts of the pre-Ch'ien-lung period (previous to 1736), collected by Teng Tuo as a fruit of his field work. The underlying significance is well brought out by Teng's own words: "It indicates that the system of *fen-ku ho-huo*, or the partnership system, was prevailing in coal mining of the time. Obviously the predominant characteristic of private capital in those days was this system.[6]

A lively spirit of partnership also features those contracts. The signatories repeatedly swore their loyalty to the partnership. Words like: "No profit was possible without partnership"; "Be one heart and one mind and one partnership forever";[7] were not untypical of their vows which sealed the contracts. They sounded remarkably like political slogans of working class solidarity, although they were non-political in nature and only involved the merchants. Yet, they were all filled with the vigour, the dream, and the spirit of partnership, the very substance that formed a new age in China.

2. Chinese Democratic Life on Seas – A Tradition of the Overseas Chinese Trade

This was the age of great political and social change. This was the age when the sea-merchant groups, especially those of Fukien and Kwangtung, rose to importance and power in Chinese history. Their rise defeated the notorious maritime interdict of Ming and early Ch'ing

---

6. Ibid.
    Teng's refreshing approach and work did break a new ground in this field. A great pity is that he only published about 20 out of his collection.
7. Ibid., p.261.
    The critics of Teng, T'ang Li and Chang interpreted *jih* as the proportion of ratio in the share of profit, which is correct. But they tended to overlook the significance of the *li-huo* or partnership system. Moreover, the extent of the government control and the importance of official accounts seem to be overstressed.

by their piracy and smuggling on the basis of the partnership system. Overseas adventure was the order of the day which highlighted a new orientation and the rising expectations of the Chinese people towards freedom and wealth. Chou Hsien-wei has noted with envy:

The wicked merchants of Fukien and Kwangtung used to have commercial intercourse with foreign countries illegally. Usually of a ship, the richest was elected as the head to loan it with cargo. The rest of the merchants followed him to overseas with their own goods and capital. The profit was so marvellous, a thousand-fold sometimes.[8]

The gazetteer of Chang-chou prefecture in the Ch'ung-chen reign (1628-44) confirmed this:

The men of Chang-chou often build great vessels and trade with foreign countries far away. Those of moderate means pool their capital and it also happens that those of means lend money for the purpose.[9]

However, as a matter of fact, the partnership system sailed with the Chinese junks overseas long before the sixteenth century. As early as the early eleventh century, it had already gone into the record of Chu Huo:

The sea vessels, the big ones had several hundreds of people and the small ones hundred over in general. The big merchants were elected as *kan-shou* or the captain, *fu-kan-shou* or vice-captain, *tsu-shih* or the administrator. They were given red seals by the maritime official, and entrusted with the power to administer justice on the ship.[10]

During that period and throughout the Sung dynasty, the Chinese overseas trade basked in the official patronage. Many measures were taken by the Sung court to encourage foreign trade. It dangled an office before any captain who could induce foreign ships with a cargo worth no less than 50,000 strings to China.[11] It provided to the foreign traders,

---

8. Chou Hsüan-wei, *Chien-lin hsü-chi* in *Han-fen lou mi-chi*, chi 8, p.37.
9. Quote Mark Elvin, p.224.
10. Chu Yü, *Ping-chou k'o-tan*, (Shanghai, 1941 rep.) p.18.
    See also Needham, Vol.4, Pt.3, p.461.
11. Kuan Li-chüan, 'The spice trade in Sung's Canton' in *SLC*, Vol.2, p.82.

apart from conceding low custom duties (only 10 per cent), big feasts on their arrivals and departures.[12] So successful was the policy that foreign trade had, from the second half of the tenth century to the twelfth century, risen from 2 per cent to 20 per cent of the annual revenue.[13]

The open-door policy was, however, abruptly ended with a ban on the overseas trade by the Ming emperor Hung-wu in 1394. Nevertheless, the maritime interdict was never effective in reality. When seduced by the great profit, the people forgot all about the ban.[14] Thus, the Ming court had to repeatedly proclaim the ban which was a virtual dead letter. Despite the death penalty, the private traders still went ahead with their overseas adventures. An early example of this was the first commercial expedition to Liu-ch'iu by some 500 private traders in 1414.[15] Everyone in the ship had a share of profit, 8 to 10 taels at the least and 30 to 40 taels at the most. The second expedition was making much smaller profit although the partners were skilled artisans. They were the reputed sea-merchants of Chang-chou and Ch'üan-chou who had long been taking the leading role in the Sino-Japanese trade ever since the Sung dynasty period.

Through piracy and smuggling, the Chinese overseas trade expanded further in the Ming dynasty. Despite its ups and downs, the expansion on the whole was on an even keel. It was on the same basis of the partnership system. But, by now, it had on board a new set of terms for the organization. For instance, the captain was no longer called *kan-shou huo-chang* and *ts'ai-fu* made their debut in Chinese history.

12. Ibid.
13. Li Chien-lung, *Sung-Yüan-Ming ching-chi shih-kao*, (a draft of the economic history of the periods of Sung, Yüan and Ming dynasties). (Peking, 1957) pp.163,166 & 170.

    I, therefore, think that the two centuries long depression of overseas trade did not actually happen. This mistake of Mark Elvin however, does not diminish the fact that his work remains a landmark for its imaginative and refreshing qualities.
14. cf. Mark Elvin, p.224.
15. Wang Chih-chen and Hsia Tse-yang, *Shih Liu-ch'iu lu* (The Mission to Liu-ch'iu), (Taipei rep., 1969) p.55.

Here we hit upon the missing link between the *k'o-chang* and *huo-chang* systems. According to *Tung-hsi-yang-k'ao*, *p'o-chu* was the captain, and *huo-chang* the navigator or pilot who had absolute command on navigation.[16]

Tung-hsi yang-k'ao speaks of the *ch'uan-chu* as the leader of the ship-merchants. But according to a Japanese source, the ship-merchants had their own leader called *k'o-chang* and *huo-chang* was the leader of the crew.[17] *Ch'uan-chu, ts'ai-fu, k'o-chang* and *huo-chang* constituted the top leadership of the shipboard organization, as well as the partnership of the ship. The seamen were all called *kung-chüeh.* This term in Nagasaki was wrongly pronounced as *kuo-sha* and in *Ch'üan-chou* where it derived from was actually called *kung-sha.*[18]

The relationship between the officers and the seacrew was remarkably democratic. As Jennifer Cushman and Tien have observed, they were not governed by a strict rule of hierarchy. Their difference was only one of responsibility.[19] Regardless of one's position and status, everyone of them called each other *hsiung-ti* or brother.[20] The essence of that tradition was that a democratic spirit of partnership and a strong sense of brotherhood were united in this calling.

*Ch'uan-shang*s or ship-merchants were the largest group in a ship which usually made up 80 per cent or more of it. They were enlisted or solicited by the captain who could benefit in many ways by having them and their cargo aboard his junk. Normally, they numbered several hundred in a reasonably big junk. They were all *k'o* or guests from everywhere in China and all came ultimately under the command of the captain. They themselves were directly under the *k'o-chang* or guest leader, who was elected by them. Smuggling and piracy had

16. Chang Hsieh, *Tung-hsi yang-k'ao* (An Investigation of the Eastern and Western Oceans), originally published 1618, (Taipei, 1962) pp.346,347.
17. Ura Ken'ichi, 'A study of Chinese Ships' in Hayashi Shunsai, ed. comp., p.16, *Kai heatai,* (Tokyo, 1958).
18. Ibid.
19. Jennifer Cushman, *Fields From The Sea* (Unpublished Ph.D. Thesis), Cornell University, 1975, p.141.
    Tien, *Shih-chi shih-chi,* in *CKCS,* Vol.3, p.280.
20. *Hsia-men-chih, 15;5.*

seasoned them as fierce and bold soldiers of fortune apart from being merchants. It was against this background that Cheng Chih-lung emerged from among them as the greatest legend in the age of romantic maritime adventurism. *K'uai-shangs* were also involved in the trade. They were the agent merchants working for some kind of specialized commercial guilds with official approval which were known as *ya-hang*. Until 1686 when foreign goods were separately taxed under *hang* tax and domestic goods under *chu* tax, there was no separation of foreign trade and domestic trade in China. The traders, either *k'o-shang* or *k'uai-shang*, engaged in both trades.[21]

They were much smaller in number than *k'o-shang* in the Chinese junk trade. A Chinese junk from Chang-chou, for example, arrived at Batavia on February 24, 1625. The *Dagh Register* speaks of 40 *quewij*s or merchants, 60 officers, and 360 passengers who came with their own goods aboard.[22] Kobata Atsuhi interprets *quewij*s as *k'uai* and the passengers as ship-merchants.[23] I think he is right. With only a few exceptions, the passengers had all been independent private traders with their own goods. *K'uai* merchants were thus the agent-merchants to be contrasted with them.

In a broader sense, the officers and crew should also be considerd as a merchant group, as they were all merchants first and sailors second.[24] All of them had a stake in the partnership. They were, in general, not paid by salaries, but allowed a certain tonnage of personal goods in the ship.

The partnership system in Fukien province was so popular that it had become a custom deeply rooted in economic life. A new term, or a

---

21. Chang Hsieh, p.279.
    P'eng Tse-i, *Ch'ing-tai kuang-tung*, 'The origin of the *hang*s for foreign trade in Canton', in *CKCS*, Vol.4, p.232.
22. Bataviasch Genootschaap Van Kunsten en Wetenschappen, *Dagh register gehouden int castell Batavia 1624-1682*, (The Hague, 1898) Vol.1, p.130.
23. Kobata Atsuhi, 'Chang-chou and Chuan-chou merchants in Ming's overseas trade' in *Toa Ronso*, 1941, Vol.4, p.140. Coincidentally or not, the Malay sea-merchants were also called *kiwi*. I think it must have connections of some sorts with the Dutch term *quewij* and Chinese term *ku'ai*. See Meilink-Roelofsz, *Asian Trade and European Influence*, (The Hague, 1962) pp.46,47.
24. Cushman, p.137; Gutzlaff, *Two Voyages*, p.46.

new standard name for firms or ships which were founded on this basis, was thus called into being:

Gathering several people to open a firm or to build a ship called *chin*. *Chin* meant combination. Such a practice was universal in Taiwan and Hsia-men.[25]

The practice was carried down to the nineteenth century in Southeast Asia by the Fukien people. Amongst those shipowners from Singapore, there were Chen Chin-chung, Chen Chin-sheng, Chin Hsieh-te, Chin I-sen, Chin Fu-tai, Chin Chang-fa, Chin Fung-fa, Chin Ching-lei, and Chin Yuan-lung. As a rule, the majority of the ships' names began with *Chin* as well.[26]

The sinkheh (Hokkien) or *hsin-k'o* system under which the penniless Chinese were recruited in large scale to overseas as cheap labour in the nineteenth century, evolved from this point. Chen Tse-hsien holds in my view correctly, that the origins of the system belong to the Ming-Ch'ing transition period or earlier. In their original form, they were the *k'o-chang* system. The system had been widely used by the Fukien and

---

25. *Hsia-men chih*, 15; 10.
26. Chen Yü-shung, 'Preface to the Chinese Tablets in Singapore' in *Nan-yang hsueh-pao*, (1971) Vol.26, No. 2, p.27.
    See Jennifer Wayne Cushman, p.148.
27. Chen Tse-hsien, *The Credit-ticket System in the 19th century*, in *CKCS*, Vol.2, p.334.
    The *Hsin-k'o* system, as a system of assisted passengers, was, according to Schaannk, already in use in West Borneo even as early as the 18th century. Some of the *Lao-k'o* or old members of small mining unions belonging to the same surnames or clans went back to China to recruit new members by assisting their passage. It was thus only natural that the assisted passengers of *hsin-k'o* joined the mining unions to which the recruiters belonged. They however had to pay back the cost of the passages to the recruiters by working in the *kongsi*-mines afterwards. They were provided with food and clothing and accommodation by the *kongsi*-mines which every 4 months paid them 16 florins each. There were however assisted passengers who owed their passages either to junk masters or to *k'o-chang (kheh-thau Hokien* (headman), who, as pointed out by the Report of the Labour Commission of 1876, were specialized recruiting agents of Chinese coolies. This, nevertheless, was a later development of the nineteenth century and generally known as the indentured labour system. See Schaannk, p.684: *Labour Commission Report* (Singapore, 1891) Purcell, pp.286,287.

Kwangtung fishermen and sea-merchants in those days. It was their practice to make a contract for the partnership. The contract included the election of the *k'o-chang* who was very often the one raising the capital, and the repayment to him with part of their profits.[27] When the *k'o-chang* system was changed and reduced to the indentured labour system, the birthmark was completely lost in the later evolution. The credit-ticket was not quite the same as the contract for partnership.

Ship-building was certainly expensive, especially for ocean vessels. For building an ocean vessel, it usually costs several tens of thousands of taels, and 4 or 5 thousand taels for the small ship.[28] Although not many could afford an ocean vessel, it was not impossible for men with small means to raise 5,000 taels either through partnership or a windfall from the overseas trade. Thus, there was a large number of captains who owned *hai-ch'uan*s or ocean vessels partially or completely. As for those who could not even have a *hai-ch'uan*, an alternative was to work for a *ts'ai-tung*, who afforded both the vessel and cargo. This kind of agent-captain was called *ch'u-hai* meaning going out to the sea.[29]

---

28. *Hsia-men Chih*, 1876.
29. Ibid.
   Chang Wei-hua interpreted *ts'ai-tung* as big bureaucrats, landlords and merchants. This was inferred from that during the reigns of Cheng-hua and Hung-chih (1465-1506), some rich and powerful families had gone abroad by big ships for overseas trade. Even with this kind of *ts'ai-tung*s, the partnership system was the standard practice. Chu Huan, the Governor of Chekiang from 1547 to 1549, testified it. According to him, overseas traders used to borrow the capital from retired officials and made use of their ships and crews. When they returned with the ships and cargoes, they first paid the original loan, calculated the interest due on the capital, and then divided the profit in equal fashion. The system had its Southeast Asian counterpart which was called *commenda*. Meilink-Roelofsz believes that the entire overseas trade of the Chinese was carried on almost exclusively in the form of *commenda*. But we should bear in mind that agent-captains and independent captains were equally numerous. And also, the biggest *ts'ai-tung*s in Chinese history such as Li Tan and Cheng Chih-lung started from scratch, and none of them were bureaucrats or landlords in origin. cf. Chang Wei-hua, *Ming-tai hai-wai Mao-i chien-lun* (A Brief Discussion on Ming's Overseas Trade) (Shanghai, 1955) pp.76,82. Mark Elvin, p.223, Meilink-Roelofsz, p.265.

Another alternative for them was to hire sea vessels such as *Hsin-hua ch'uan*s which were rented at a rate of 80 taels each.[30] The merchants of Fen-ping, Chien-ling, Shao-wu and Ting-chu prefectures frequently hired them to smuggle out to sea. They loaded the logs above, and the silk and cotton underneath.

The enormous success of the Chinese overseas trade had drained a great many marine talents into this channel. A Ming official started to complain about this:

> Good mariners found it more attractive to work in the private junks for they offered much handsomer pay and higher profits. On the contrary, the government's pay was so meagre, scarcely 6 taels, which made them very unhappy to serve the government. Moreover, the government ship barely made one trip in several years and yet they were prohibited to do their own trade. Therefore when the government recruited them, all of the best mariners went into hiding. Despite the government attempt to round them up, only those incompetent mariners were caught.[31]

Too little pay and too much restrictions had been the cause for the so-called talent-drain. Yet, what the Ming and Ch'ing court did was to suppress private participation in the overseas trade, either by heavy taxation or total ban. Monopoly was their primary aim and when impossible, control. All through the rugged years of suppression, the private overseas trade was thriving on the unchecked flow of talents, piracy and smuggling.

From the start, economic inequality was inevitable in the partnership system. Some partners might get more and some less in the share of profit. Already in the mid-fifteenth century, the rich families who afforded the capital to buy the cargo, reaped full harvest of profits. On the other hand, the poor could only make a living out of it.[32] However, as the overseas trade could yield profit over tenfold, it provided a ladder to wealth. But this kind of commercial adventurism was very hazardous and unpredictable:

30. MCSL:YP, pem 7, p.618.
31. Wang Shih-chen, *Shih-hsueh-chi*, p.35.
32. Chang Hsieh, p.266.

Suddenly rich and suddenly poor, it was so easy to rise and fall.[33]

In the later centuries, inequality in the profit-sharing had grown more marked in the *ch'uan-chu* system. Crawfurd has taken note of it in a Chinese junk of 8,000 piculs in weight:[34]

POSITION	INCOME
1. *ch'uan-chu* (captain)	100 piculs
p'o-chu	+ $100-$200 (passage fees)
	10% commission on the net profits of the voyage
2. *huo-chang* (navigator)	50 piculs
	$200 (salary)
3. *ts'ai-fu*	50 piculs
	$100
4. captain of the steerage	15 piculs of freight
5. captains of the anchor	9 piculs each
6. seaman	7 piculs

Although the economic inequality kept growing wider and wider within the system, until early in the nineteen century, the shipboard organization still retained its democratic features. As late as 1831, the 'democracy' still made a profound impression on Gutzlaff:

> In fact, the sailors exercise full control over the vessel, and oppose every measure with which they think may prove injurious to their own interests; so that even the captain and pilot are frequently obliged, when worn out with their insolent behaviour, to crave their kind assistance, and to request them to show a better temper.[35]

The 'democracy' seemed to Gutzlaff to amount to a reign of anarchy:

> All of them, however stupid, are commanders and if anything of importance to be done, they bawl out their command to each other till all is utter confusion.[36]

33. *Hsia-men chih*, 15:5.
34. John Crawfurd, *Journey of an Embassy to the Chinese Courts of Siam and Cochin-China* (Kuala Lumpur, 1967), originally published in 1828, p.412.
35. Gutzlaff C., *Journal of Three Voyages* (London, 1838) pp.83,84.
36. Ibid.

The picture of them as without leadership may be exaggerated, but here the picture certainly reflects that democracy in the Chinese junks was a way of life.

In a comparison of the Western route to capitalism, Dr. Tien blames the partnership system for the retarded growth of Chinese capital.[37] The blame is unfounded and biased. As a matter of fact, owing to the system, the Chinese overseas trade went from strength to strength. The accelerated expansion gave rise to the Cheng maritime commercial empire.

A new era of merchant power emerged with the Cheng empire. Old China was stormed by many peasant uprisings but when they were gone new dynasties cropped up in their trail. The old feudal rule remained. In the Ming dynasty period there began a change. Now it was the merchant protest movements which raged angrily. They added a new form of struggle – general strikes and demonstrations – in the fight against feudal courts and rule. But, such storms were merely the explosions of the merchants or handicraft workers when wronged or overtaxed by the authorities. Their achievements were less impressive than the peasant uprisings in term of a larger scale or a change of dynasty. Only the Cheng regime climaxed the changes. It was the first time in Chinese history that the merchant groups had ever achieved power, a power which was based on the partnership system instead of the imperial system.

---

37. Tien, p.280.

Chapter 3

THE FUKIEN SEA-MERCHANT KINGDOMS AND THE HAKKA MINER SELF-GOVERNMENT

1. *Kongsi* in the Sea-merchant Kingdoms

A rising tide of *wo-k'ou* or 'Japanese piracy' in 1527 began to invade the coastal provinces. It was indeed an uprising of Chinese sea-merchants who could find no way out but revolt against the increasingly tightened ban on overseas trade. Most of them were mainly from Linchou, Shaohsing, Chang-chou and Chuan-chou, from Fukien province.[1] Less than 10 per cent of them were actually Japanese. The revolt of sea-merchants gained momentum after 1541 as the ban became more severe.[2] More and more seafarers joined Hsü Tung who led the revolt.

---

1. Kobata Atsuhi, "A study of the history of Medieval Sino-Japanese Trade", p.496.
    The need of redefining the so-called *wo'k'ou* (Japanese piracy) has so long been overdue. Happily, efforts to correct the conventional bias have been started. As early as 1955, S. Katayama correctly identified them as the independent merchants who were not under the economical control of the coastal gentry. They fought for the abolition of the maritime ban which was the root of the revolts. So Kuan-wai contributes much of the devastation of the questionable term *wo* in Chinese history, but leaves *k'ou* there untouched.
    Seijiro Katayama, in Toyo Shigaku Ronshu, Vol.4, (Tokyo 1955) p.426.
    So Kuan-wai, *Japanese Piracy in Ming China During 16th Century*, (New York, 1975) pp.212-217.
2. Ibid., p.493.
3. So is sympathetic to Wang Chih and his close associates. He says: "An objective perusal of his stories shows that he was particularly interested in securing in legalization of trade between the ordinary Chinese people and foreign traders, that is, trade outside the tribute system. He had given the official all kinds of cooperation, such as the suppression of those pirates who obstructed trade, before he allowed himself to be placed in the hands of Hu Tsung-hsien. The same may applied to Wang's associates, such as Mao Hai-feng and Hsü Ch'uan.". Yet, they remain in his eyes pirates. So. p.34.

After Hsü Tung was killed by the Ming forces, Wang Chih, who had served as *kuan-kuei*, the accountant, then a military chief under Hsü, was elected to the leadership. Wang Chih was a man of Anhwei. He was reputed for his heroism in his youth and distinguished himself as an expert in tactics and strategy when he turned adult.[3] From 1540 to 1545, Wang Chih and his close friends, Yeh Chung-man, Hsü Wei-hsüeh and so on entered a partnership in overseas trade. They built a big vessel in Kuangtung and smuggled out gunpowder and silk to Japan, Thailand and other parts of Southeast Asia.[4] Wang amassed a great fortune through this means. The Japanese thus admired and respected him and called him *Wu-feng-chuanchü*. *Ch'uan-chu* or *P'o-chu* in this context was the title used by the captain of all captains, by someone like Kapitan China. Thus, when Wang succeeded Hsü, he was elected as the *Po-chu* to lead the whole fleet of Hsü's vessels.[5]

Wang Chih became crowned with unchallenged power in the sea after he had eliminated his rival sea lord, Chen Shih-ting. All the private sea vessels from then on sailed under his flag. Wang Chih, the founder of this powerful seabourne empire, claimed to be the king who clears the sea, *Chin-hai-Wang* and established his own government to rival the Ming court. Under his protection, foreign ships could freely visit and leave China and foreign trade traders did their business in Su-chou and Hang-chou openly without fear.[6] Streams of people offered rice and wine or even their own sons or daughters to Wang's fleet.[7] Even the local defence officials also sent red blankets and jade belts as presents to Wang.

The tides of *wo-k'ou* eventually subsided in 1567. Whether it had learnt a lesson or not, the Ming court, however, did relax the maritime ban and introduced the licence system for overseas trade on the recommendation of the governor of Fukien. However, Wang Chih had blazed the trail for the later builders of maritime empires in the early 17th century such as Kapitan Li Tan, Cheng Chih-lung and Cheng Ch'eng-

---

4.   Ibid.
5.   *Wen-tai Wo-chi*, Vol.1, *wo-pien* 2 in *Hsuan Lan-tang ch'ung shu hsu chi*, Vol.15.
6.   Fan Puei, Shai-k'ou i-chien in *Hsuan Lan-tang ch'ung shu hsu chi*, Vol.15.
7.   Ibid., p.2

kung. All of them personified the age of overseas adventurism. Before Wang Chih and his partners launched their partnership in overseas trade, he said to them: "The law in China is far too severe and inhibitive. It is almost impossible to do anything without offending the law at all. Why don't we go overseas to enjoy the vast freedom?"[8] These

8 Fan Puei, *Hai-k'ou i-k'uo* op.cit., p.1.
   Many historians are misled by Chu Huan into a belief that the local gentry and officials were the greatest organizers and protectors of the massive smuggling. Actually, the local gentry and official played only the supporting role. For example, see Mark Elvin, p.222.
   On the other hand, totally a biased history still, Hucker's article tags a label 'raiders' to the rebelling sea-merchants. This is also very misleading, which no doubt will leave us with the impression that the so-called *wo-kou* were indeed pirates. A contemporary record, *Ch'ou-hai t'u-p'ien* has some kinder words to say about them:

   "Since the *shih-po* was lifted in the early Chia-ching...piracy has become common. Why? It is because pirates and merchants are the same group of people. When trade is permitted, pirates become merchants. When trade is prohibited, merchants convert to pirates. The law was originally aimed at suppressing the commercial activity. But now it mainly deals with piracy. Rather than becoming better, the piracy is getting more notorious."

   It is about time that history should clear their name.
   Charles O. Hucker, 'Hu Tsung-hsien's campaign against Hsü Hai, 1556' in Kierman and Fairbank ed., *Chinese Ways in Warfare*, (New York, 1974) pp.304-7.
   Ng Chin-keong, 'Gentry-Merchant and Peasant-peddlers – The Response of the South Fukienese to the Offshore Trading Opportunities 1552-1566' in *Nanyang Tahsüeh-pao* (Singapore, 1973) Vol.7, p.167.

9. Iwao Seiichi, 'Li Tan, Chief of the Chinese Residents at Hirado' in Toyogakuho Vol.23, p.395.
    C.R. Boxer. 'The Rise and Fall of Nicholas Iquan' in *Tien-hsia* monthly, 11.1;402,3. The life of Captain Li Tan is still surrounded with mystery. All that we can establish is that he was a man of Chuan-chou, who had established himself in Manila as a Chinese leader but lost all his fortune to the value of 40,000 taels to the Spaniards who put him in jail. However, he made his escape to Japan where he became the China Captain respected by both overseas Chinese and foreigners. At Nagasaki and Hirado, he had magnificent houses and pretty wives. By that time he was so wealthy that he loaned 60,000 taels, a great sum of money to Feudal Lord Shimazu. As opposed against the mainland Chinese, he was already Christianized, or at least taking Christian name, Andrea Dittis. His children were also given Christian names. See Seiichi Iwao, 'Li Tan, Chief of the Chinese Residents at Hirado, Japan in the Last Days of the Ming Dynasty' in *Memoirs of the Research Department of the Toyo Bunko*, Tokyo, No.17. 1958.

words must have found a reverberation in the hearts of hundreds of thousands of sea-merchants and seafaring people.

In the 1610s, a maritime commercial empire of Kapitan China, Li Tan, emerged from his fleet of Chinese junks busily cruising to and from Japan, Taiwan, P'eng-hu, Vietnam, Thailand, Cambodia, Manila and Batavia.[9] In his capacity as the most influential overseas Chinese leader, he had acted as the intermediary for the British and Dutch to open up official commercial intercourse with China.[10] Despite his good offices, the Ming official records still slandered him as traitor, pirate, bandit and so on.[11] In fact, he would never sacrifice the interest of Chinese sea-merchants in his efforts to bring about liberal policy in foreign trade. It is proven by his refusal to accept the Dutch proposal to end all Chinese junk trade with Manila in the negotiation of 1624.[12]

His commercial empire was also founded upon the partnership system. At the beginning of his partnership, there were 28 people altogether. They were Hsi Hsin-su, the Dutch agent-merchant who had gone to jail for Li, Yang Tien-sheng, a ship captain, and Hong Sheng and Chang Hung and Cheng Chih-lung, all sworn brothers, and overseas traders in Japan. Captain Li Tan was their leader and Cheng Chih-lung ranked the last because he was the youngest.[13]

---

10. Iwao Seiichi, pp.412-415.
11. Ibid.
12. *Dagh Register, gehouden int castell Batavia 1624-1682* (The Hague, 1888) Vol.1, p.143, April9 1624, p.140.
13. *Shen Yün, T'ai-wan Cheng-shih shih-mo* (Complete Record of the Cheng Taiwan) TW, no.15, p.1.2.
14. Hua Chun, *Tung Wan* (Reminiscence) 1;35 in *Shih-yen ts'ung-shu*, 11;1.
     The early life of Cheng chi-lung was as much mysterious as that of Captain China. We are told that while he was a broker of the Portuguese in Macao, he was baptized. He then migrated to Japan and worked for Captain Li Tan. Soon his commercial ability and fidelity won complete trust from Li Tan and his partners who entrusted him with more and more valuable cargoes to Cambodia and overseas. After Li Tan's death, he succeeded to the leadership of Li's maritime empire not without opposition from Li's eldest son Ausustin 1625. However, in 1627, his forces was said to have consisted of almost 400 junks and 60,000 to 70,000 men.
     Seiichi Iwao, pp.71-79.
     Wu Fa's *Taiwan Li-shih Cha-chi* (Hong Kong, 1976) is an interesting and informative account of the Cheng Regime, although limited to Chinese sources.

Li Tan presided over a maritime empire comprised of ten branches or *ts'ais*. Each ts'ai was autonomous and headed by one of his partners. They were respectively called *jen*, kindness, *i*, loyalty, *li*, ceremony, *chih*, intelligence, *hsin*, honesty, *chin*, gold, *mu*, wood, *shui*, water, *huo*, fire, *t'u*, earth.[14] These *ts'ais* were renamed *hang*s when Cheng Chih-lung succeeded Li Tan. As they were called *hang*s, Kuo Mo-jo, the leading historian in China, has considered them as commercial firms. He admits that he is unable to find out what these *hang*s were all about. In his own words: "Where were these *hang*s established and what kind of business were they dealing with? It is regretted that there is no detailed material for a further investigation. I have consulted many experts but even they themselves do not have a clue."[15] It seems to be a deadlock here.

Fortunately, all these problems can be solved. These *hang*s were neither commercial guilds nor firms in the ordinary sense. As they were in part piratical and in part commercial, these *hang*s were involved in a very intensive coastal and overseas trade on the one hand and collected protection fees from Chinese junks on the other. Nevertheless, piracy or protection fees was only their sideline business. The ticket fee or protection fee demanded by them for each junk was said to have been a thousand taels.[16] Cheng Chih-lung is said to have demanded 3,000 taels from each junk as ticket fee. His wealth was, therefore, as rich as a nation.[17]

It is evidently an exaggeration, for even ocean vessels normally carried cargo of no more than tens of thousands of taels. Li Chih-chi, who refused to surrender to the Ming court and broke away from Cheng Chih-lung, charged ticket fees according to the size of the junk. The fees varied from 20 to 50 taels.[18] I think it is the standard practice not only carried out by Li's *ts'ai* but also by Cheng's regime which comprised 10 *hang* or *ts'ai*. As Li Tan and Cheng Chih-lung were never regarded as merchants but pirates by official Chinese historians,

15. Kuo Mo-jo, *CKCS*, Vol.3, p.124.
16. Hua Chun, 1;35.
17. Li Yao, *To-shih shih-i* in *MCSLCP*, p.1576.
18. *MCSL:IP*, 7;618.

it was no surprise that they spread the myth that Li and Cheng derived their wealth from ticket fees.

The Cheng regime was from first to last a maritime commercial empire which was supported by his armada to control the South China Sea. Overseas and coastal trade were its lifeline. The regime participated in Asian and Southeast Asian trade on a scale that rivalled the .V.O.C. Especially in Japan, the Dutch lost out to the Cheng regime. Cheng Chih-lung derived great profits from Sino-Japanese trade by concentrating his capital on big ocean ships and valuable goods such as silk. In 1641, six of his ships imported 90,920 *fan* of fine silk into Nagasaki whereas 91 other Chinese junks only 44,016 *fan*.[19] Seven of his ships and 34 other Chinese ships visited Nagasaki in 1643, his ships accounted for one third of the total import by Chinese junks.[20] Two of his ships in 1644 carried a cargo of 250,000 taels to Japan.[21] By contrast, generally a sea junk could load a cargo no more than 30,000 taels.

Also, Cheng's partnership conducted a brisk and intense commercial traffic with Southeast Asian countries. In 1655 alone 24 of their trading junks were sent to countries all over Southeast Asia. Seven set sail to Batavia, two to Tokyo, ten to Thailand, four to Vietnam and one to Manila. The crucial importance of overseas trade to the survival of the Cheng regime was highlighted by Cheng Ch'eng-kung himself:

> The coastal areas are securely in our hands and we derived our fund from overseas trade. These advantages will place us in a position that we can either advance or retreat easily.[22]

The military forces of the Cheng regime comprised 400,000 men and 5,000 junks. The economic basis for this enormous military strength was the large scale participation of one regime in coastal and

19. Yamawaki Daijiro, *Nagasaki no To-jin boeki* (Chinese Trade at Nagasaki) (Tokyo, 1964) p.30.
20. Ishihra Michihiro, 'Cheng Chih-lung's overseas trade in Japan and Southeast Asia', in *Minami Asia Gakuho*, no. 1, pp.162-8.
21. Iwao Seiichi, 'Japan's foreign relations in early modern period' in Iwanami Koza, Nihon Rekishi, Vol.15, pp.60,61.
22. Yang Ying, *Ts'ung-cheng shih-lu* 'Records of following the campaigns of Coxinga' (Peking, 1931 rep.) p.35.

overseas trade. The regime was reinforced by more and more rich merchants who joined in with their own capital. In May 1647, the *Dagh Register des comptoirs Nagasque* entered this:

> Today, we heard that Iquan's son and his brothers led 700 small junks and a large army in Pescadores. There were many rich merchants who brought great sums of money and goods to join them.[23]

Cheng's commercial empire was a partnership complex which put out ten branches or *hangs*. All of them in charge of *hu-kuan* Cheng Tai, the treasurer. Five of them, *jen* (kindness), *i* (loyalty), *li* (ceremony), *chih* (intelligence), *hsin* (honesty), *hangs* were Hsia-men based and other five Hang-chou based. Cheng Tai was the house-manager in Cheng's family. With his outstanding ability as a financier or manager, he gradually became the most prominent partner and minister to Coxinga.[24]

Coxinga had such a complete trust in him that he put all his money at the disposal of Cheng Tai. Chai Cheng who had gone to Japan to claim Cheng Tai's money for Coxinga's son, Cheng Ching, testifies it as follows:

> The coastal areas of Fukien province annually paid tax to Coxinga in rice or money which were collected by Cheng Tai. He sent the ships overseas. On return, the Chuan-chus, the captains, had to return the loan money with interest to him. Not even a single cent was kept in Coxinga's house. Daily necessities including rice, logs, tea, candles, clothes were all handled by him. The whole of Hsia-men knew about it.[25]

It was no strange thing that Coxinga left all his money in the hands of Cheng Tai, his most trusted *huo-chi*. This was entirely in the tradition of the *huo-chi* system prevalent in his time.

What was new was the relationship between the King and his ministers, which was based on partnership. Cheng Tai, a millionaire him-

23. Quote Ura Ken'ichi, 'Yen-p'ing-wang hu-kuan' in *T'ai-wan Feng-wu* (March, 1961) p.30.
24. Ibid., p.32
25. Ibid.

self, was the No.2 man in the Cheng regime in which he headed the ministry of treasury, *hu-pu*. There was 15 officials who served under him, 2 *shih-lang*, 4 *lang-chung* and 8 *chi-shih*.[26] Apart from the population tax, coastal and overseas trade also fell into the realm of the ministry.

The ministry had framed a 'nation'-wide network of capital investment in coastal and overseas trade. Merchants were enlisted to become business partners of the Cheng regime which supplied them the capital at low interest. The famous five big merchants who established their business in Peking, Su-chou, Hang-chou, Shantung and other places, were Cheng's partners.[27] They apparently belonged to the Hang-chou based *chin* (gold), *mu* (wood), *shui* (water), *huo* (fire) and *tu* (earth) *hang*s. One of them in 1656 or a bit later was arrested by the Ch'ing government.

Chen Ting-lao was arrested. Cheng had been supplied with capital at a monthly rate of one candureen three cash per tael by the Cheng regime, through the *kuan-ku* (treasurer) Wu I-sheh, the treasurer. Each time after the business transaction was over, he had to return the loan money plus interest before he could have another loan. He had received 50,000 taels from the *kuan-ku* in early May 1654 and the money was used by him to buy a ship of cargo which was to sell in Japan. In November of the same year, after settling the old account, he had a fresh loan of 100,000 taels. Then, in 1655, he paid back 60,000 taels in term of silvers and a cargo of silk. The rest was given by the Cheng regime for the use of spying and rallying support for the anti-Manchu cause.[28]

The *hu-pu*, the treasury department of the Cheng regime, acted as a financial bank of some sort to finance private investments. This contrasted with the Ming and Ch'ing courts which did everything to kill private incentive. This, and only this made the Cheng regime a revolutionary breakthrough in the economic functions of Chinese govern-

---

26. *Cheng-shih kuan-hsi wen-shu* (Documents on relations with the Cheng family) T.W., no.69., p.4.
27. *MCSL:TP*, 3;215.
28. Ibid.

ments. The *hu-pu* as such functioned as a government bank which operated on the basis of the partnership system.

Yet, Chen, who had a partnership of his own, was undoubtedly one of the big partners of the Cheng regime. His partnership had been stemming from Cheng's partnership complex, although it somehow maintained separate accounts and autonomy. There were about 8 people in his partnership to share the capital which was supplied by the Cheng regime. They were Wu Ch'i-lian, Chen Hsiao-wu, Kho Wen-lao, Chen Mao-fen and Huang Sun-lian.[29] The same was true of all Cheng's partners, including Cheng Tai and the other four big merchants who were linked with the regime through partnership. Each of them was an independent partnership in itself, although the Cheng regime acted as their supplier of finance. Hsi Shao-fang, Yen Tuan and Fu Ts'en-i were three of the four famous big merchants whose names have come to light.[29]

Though Cheng Tai served Cheng Chih-lung and Coxinga faithfully, he also had his own ships and partnership within the Cheng commercial empire. He had banked his own money 300,000 taels in Japan before Hsia-men was lost. He did not deposit the money himself but through his partners; Kung Erh-lian, Hung Wei-she, Chang Shih-kuan, Cheng Ping-kuan and Hung Tuo-lian who brought it in several instalments.[30] After his death, both his descendants and Cheng Ching, (whose life was saved by Cheng Tai but who in return accused Cheng Tai for treachery which caused his death), disputed over the banked money. Cheng Ching's claim was represented by Chai Cheng in the above-mentioned quotation. But, it was only one side of the coin and the declaration of Kung Erh-lian revealed the other side:

> In the past, both Coxinga and Ti-ya (Cheng Tai) had their own junks sent overseas. Sometimes, Coxinga and his cargoes attached to Ti-ya's ships, in which case he had his agents to follow the ships. They also had different names for their own business concerns. It was called Tien Huang for Coxinga and Tung Li for Ti-ya. Thus, all the

29. *Cheng-shih Kuan-hsi Wen-shu*, pp.19,20.
30. Ura Ken'ichi, pp.44-47.
31. Ura Ken'ichi, pp.100,101.

45

previously deposited money were kept in the cases which bore the name of Tung Li.[31]

Such evidence as there is proves beyond doubt that the Cheng regime constituted a radical alternative to the Ming and Ch'ing courts because it was founded on the partnership system. Politically, Cheng Tai served the Cheng regime as the minister of treasury like a servant serving his master. But the partnership system removed the servant-master relationship between them economically. So far as the business concerns went, Cheng Tai was an equal partner to the Cheng family whose role was no more than supplying capital with interest. It therefore becomes abundantly clear that each branch of Cheng's maritime commercial empire was an autonomous partnership in itself.

At the grass-root level, each ship was a partnership. The partnership system served to cement *chuan-chu*s, officers and sailors in their loyalty to the Cheng Kingdom. Two trading junks of the Cheng regime which were captured by the Ch'ing officials in Hsia-men confirmed this. The ships carried a great variety of goods in large volume from Taiwan to Japan and Thailand in 1683. The ship under captain Huang Ch'eng belonged to an official of Cheng's government service board, Hung Lei, who had then already surrendered to the Ch'ing court. Captain Lan Cheh's ship was owned by an earl of Cheng's regime, *Wu-p'ing Hou* Liu Kuo-hsüan. The surviving official record has given a complete name list of all the officers and crew members in the ship under captain Huang Cheng. It has also listed in full the items of cargo in the ship.[32] There were 67 persons altogether including officers and sailors, and according to the name list given, 23 officers and 44 sailors or *Mu-shao*. After going through the name list, the record clearly distinguishes the cargoes into 3 categories; 1. the *kongsi*'s cargo, 2. the attached cargo and 3. the sailors' or *mu-shaos*' cargo.[33] The *kongsi* cargo here is, I think, that which belonged to all the officers who shared it together. The attached cargo may have been belonged to the Cheng

---

32. *MCSL:TP*, 3;298
33. Ibid.

family, or more likely to Hung Lieh himself, the shipowner, or to both and others.

The use of the term *kongsi* in referring to the whole body of ship officers heralded the use of it in calling all officers in the mines of Bangka and West Borneo where the earliest Chinese *kongsi* emerged. *Kongsi* as a form of self-government and partnership had long existed in Chinese grass-root democracy in the Chinese mines and sea-junks since the 15th century or probably earlier. All that was lacking is the term *kongsi* for the belated recognition of this fact. And now there it is, the earliest appearance of the term *kongsi* in Chinese history!

2. A Migration of Hakka Mining Traditions

> Gold borne by the earth,
> Riches hidden in mountains,
> Only hard work can earn us,
> A livelihood from mines.
>
> *– Lo Fang-po*

Most of the Chinese in West Borneo were Hakka. The Lan-fang *kongsi* which was situated in Mandor and the neighbouring districts had a majority of the Chia-ying Hakka. But before 1777, they were not the majority. The miners there had been largely the Chao-chou Hakka, dominantly in the mines of Mao-ern-shan, Chu-ta-ya, Kun-jih, Lung-kung and Senaman. But at Ming-huang and its nearby areas, the Ta-p'u and Kang-chou Hakka were in the majority.[34]

In the Chinese districts in Sambas, such as Singkawang, Montrado, Lara, Loemar, and Sepang, the Hui-chou Hakka forged the overwhelming majority.[35] Two largest *kongsi*, Ta-kang (the great port) and San-t'iao-kuo (the three ditches), were both under their control. Although in the pioneering days, the Chia-ying Hakka had been working gold mines in Montrado, in between 1772 and 1774 part of them were driven away. Thereafter, the Hui-chou Hakka firmly entrenched their power and government in Montrado. However, shortly after

---

34. Lo, p.137.
35. Schaannk, p.515.

1825, the Chia-ying Hakka did make a comeback, but no longer in agriculture or mining. They went into the business of smuggling salt, opium and gunpowder between Mandor and Bengkajang.[36]

The Chao-chou Hakka in West Borneo were a small number among the Chinese. Those Chao-chou Hakka who lived in mining settlements were mainly traders. A slightly larger number of them consisting of traders, farmers, handicraft workers and seamen could be found in Pontianak and the adjacent areas.[37] Very few Hokkien migrated to West Borneo. Only in Pontianak was there a small number of Hokkien inhabiting the town.[38]

In West Borneo and elsewhere in Southeast Asia, the Hakka or the guest people were almost singularly the miners now and well into the nineteenth century. The Hokkien and Cantonese were traders overseas. This occupational pattern was created by history. The Hokkien and Cantonese had, ever since the fifteenth century, established their leading roles in overseas trade, the crowning achievement of which were the emergence of sea-merchant kingdoms during the Ming-Ch'ing transition period. As the latecomers in the seas, the Hakka found that while the others had made fields from the sea, they be better able to make their own from the mines. It was not because there was a lack of talent and skill of the Hakka in overseas trade, but because in the field of mining their ancestral experience and passion could assure them a leading role.

In their homeland, the Hakka were reputed passionate miners for centuries.

Chia-ying chou, where the Chia-ying Hakka came from, a mountainous and barren country, had produced a breed of freedom loving people, among them the men of Taiping, including Hung Hsiü-chuan. Many scholars, merchants, miners sprang from its soil. It is said that the Chia-ying people lived on nothing else but studies alone in Sung times.[39] But in the Ch'ing period, the Chia-ying scholars had to make teaching their living but even this was increasingly difficult in the

36. Schaannk, p.514.
37. Ibid.
38. Schaannk, p.515.
39. *Chia-ying chou-chi*, 8:1.

eighteenth and nineteenth century. Many of them, as Wen Chung-ho observed, had already looked upon Nanyang or Southeast Asia as their second home.[40]

For example, the founders of the Lan-fang *kongsi*, Lo Fang-po, Ku Liu-po and Liu Tai-erh all came from a long line of scholars in their families. Descending from a family tradition of studies wedded with farming, Lo Fang-po was born in Shih-shan-pou (castle of stone fan), an outlying village forty miles away from the city.[41] He was thus brought up with the old classic as well as martial arts. Liu Tai-erh, the fifth kapitan of the Lan-fang *kongsi*, came from Pai-tu-pou of Chia-ying chou, being reared with the similar family tradition which was indeed the Hakka way of life.[42] His successor, Ku Liu-po, was from a prominent clan in Chia-ying chou. Ku clan was brought into prominence by the literary fame of its descendants.[43]

It was the Hakka way of life that "the women worked in the fields, at building houses, at porterage, while the men, cutlass or spear in hand, watched for enemies or went fighting."[44] The Hakka men studied for degree while their wives worked in the farms. Eighty per cent of the Hakka women were the tillers of the soil whereas only twenty per cent of the Hakka men were farmers. The men turned to handicraft and business, scholarship and mining, and adventures in other lands.[45] So they were least tied down by the land, when the distant call of opportunity reached them, they shipped off to the South Seas, or went away as peddlers, or dug for gold in foreign soil.

Since overseas mining asserted a strong fascination on the Hakka, the scholars and the others alike turned their eyes to the land of promise across the ocean. Lo Fang-po wrote of himself and his migration to West Borneo in a poem:[46]

---

40. *Chia-ying chou-chi* 8:1
41. Lo, pp.33,65,66.
42. Lo, p.79.
43. Lo, p.80.
44. Han Suyin, *The Crippled Tree*, (London, 1965) p.27.
45. Lo Hsian-lin, *K'o-Chai Shih-liao Hui-pien*, (Hong Kong, 1965) pp.16,17.
46. Lo, p.148.

> I turned myself from a scholar to merchant,
> Not worrying million miles of journey,
> I travelled like a lotus leaf without a home.

Many, however, were miners or handicraft workers at home before their migration to West Borneo. Chia-ying chou itself boasted of a wealth of silver, lead, coal and iron ores. Wen Chung-ho was proud of its natural resources in the past:[47]

> Chen-hsian (Chia-ying chou was named Chen-hsian in Ming times) was renowned for its silkworm which was sold all over China. Its silver mines, lead mines, coal mines and iron mines were all rich in the wood.

The origin of Hakka mining traces back to the sixteenth century. By 1553, there had already 23 iron process tanks or *lu* established in Hui-chou by private merchants. The local government levied a tax of 10 taels per tank per year.[48] This private iron mining and processing had been blessed with official approval. But private participation in silver mining was prohibited by the Ming government which made it a government monopoly. This monopoly policy sparked off endless miner uprisings.

One which took place in Hui-chou in 1560, involved tens of thousands of illegal Hakka miners. They occupied the silver mines between Ch'ang-lo and Hai-feng by force. The official history labelled them as *hao-min* (powerful people) or *chien-min* (cunning people). This kind of people, such as Wu Tuan, Lung Ti, Hsieh Fi-hu were the miner leaders who like Teng Mao-chi and Yeh Chung-liu arose from obscure backgrounds and proclaimed themselves kings. There were several hundred groups of miners, each varying from a few hundreds to two or three thousands, each under the standard of a self-proclaimed king. They had 'ravaged' the countryside of Hsin-lin, Ch'ang-lo, Chieh-yang, Ho-yuen, Lung-chuan, Po-lo, Ku-shan and Hai-feng.[49]

---

47. *Chia-ying Chou-chi*, Preface, 2, 32;14.
48. *Hui-chou fu-chi*, 17;21.
49. *Hui-chou fu-chi*, 17;22.

Their true identity as miner was obscured by the passage of time, but more so by the ritualistic distortion and slander of the official history. They were branded as 'bandit' by the Ming authorities which eventually put the uprising down in 1570.[50] However, reports of Hakka illegal mining kept flowing. A report that the unsettled people from Po-lo hsien illegally opened tin mines again appeared in 1620.[51] Another report came in 1626 that in the mountains of Ch'ang-lo the illegal tin miners grew increasingly aggressive.[52] In 1640, at the end of the Ming dynasty, Po-lo hsien was ravaged by another storm of miner uprising.[53]

> At first, the bandits who occupied tin mines by force kept a low profile by pretending that they were there doing nothing but farming. Soon, they gathered hundreds and thousands of lawless elements. Oath or *yüeh* was made to bind themselves into a brotherhood named *Ch'ang-hsin* (eternal prosperity). The brotherhood seized any good farm land that came to its notice, but refused to be taxed by the government. They destroyed graveyards, occupied farms in the mining area. Lawless miners even appropriated the land rents or taxes of the government and landlords. In resistance to official arrest, they burnt down houses (which by implication should be landlords' residence and government office). So formidable were they that they not only dared to arrest landlords and police officials but also to repel or kill the soldiers who had come to interfere with them.

This probably was the earliest official record of the Hakka miner brotherhood and self-government. A century later, we also hear of a revival of Hakka miner brotherhoods in Yünnan and Kwanghsi. The copper miners in Yünnan had been described by Lin Tse-hsü, the

50. Chü Ta-chin, *Kuantung hsin-yu,* 7;36.
51. *Hui-chou fu-chi,* 17;43.
52. *Hui-chou fu-chi,* 17;44.
53. *Hui-chou fu-chi,* 17;22.
   AT opposite ends of the intellectual spectrum in the interpretation of Chinese bandits, Chesneaux and Hobsbawm are sitting on the left and Metzger on the right. While the former romanticized Chinese social bandits, the latter vulgarized them. See Eric Hobsbawm, *Bandits* (New York, 1969) p.64.
   Thomas A. Metzger, 'Chinese Bandits: The Traditional Perception Re-Evalued' in JAS Vol.xxxiii, No.3, May 1974, p.455.

governor of Yünnan and Kui-chou, as mostly rough and cunning people:[54]

> The custom of forming brotherhoods was very popular in mines. It was a saying in Yünnan that no mines could be founded without an oath of brotherhood. Their conflicting interest sometimes tore them apart. However, they joined together to strengthen their position and control in the area. Gradually, they began to defy the law and authorities there. Thus, in mining districts, not only the officials were worried about not to interfere with them, but also the local gentry and residents were in great awe and keeping a wary eye on them.

The Yünnan copper miners included not only the impoverished Yünnanese, but also those coolies from Kwangtung, Kwanghsi and others provinces.[55] A significant portion of them must have been the Hakka who always pioneered the trails of mines in China and overseas.

In the mid-Eighteenth century, for example, the Hakka miners brought a boom of silver mining to Vietnam. They had established the Sung-hsing (delivering stars) mining settlement in which they had their own rules and shops and medical practitioners. Their organization was also the *k'o-chang* system, similar to that in Yünnan. One of the *k'o-chang* there, Chang Te-yi came from Ch'ang-lo county of Kwangtung in 1761. After working for a while as coolie, he was selected by his own group of miners as the *k'o-chang*.[56] However, large parts of the miners there had been the Ch'ao-chou natives and Chao-chou Hakka, estimated tens of thousands in total.[57] Each of the mining brotherhoods such as Chang's and his rival's, was led by seven *chang* or heads with an average of two to three hundred men in its membership.[58]

Hakka miners brotherhoods also found their way to Kwanghsi during the reign of Tao-kuang (1821-1850) or earlier. In Kuei county,

54. *CKCTSKS*, p.340.
55. *CKCTSKS*, p.339.
56. *Shih-liao shün-k'ang* (Taiwan rep. 1963) p.425.
57. Tatsuro Yamamoto ed., (History of International Relations between Vietnam and China), (Tokyo, 1975) p.431.
58. *Shih-liao*, op.cit., p.425.

the cradle of the Taiping revolution, the Hakka coal miners were said to have come from Chia-ying after 1723.[59] The opening of silver mines by the local magistrate in 1819 began the influx of Hakka miners from everywhere in China. The influx continued during the reign of Tao-kuang when the successive magistrate revived private mining. A stone tablet dated 1887 speaks of the migration of Hakka miner brother-hood:[60]

> Rascals continued to come in flocks. Within one or two years, the deep valleys as well as the remote mountains had all been inhabited by the *yu-min* (the wandering people). They were strong, muscular, single and very fierce and violent. They committed all sorts of crimes; robbery, plunder and founding brotherhoods. The local police dared not go into mines to interfere.

Hakka miners in Kuei county, coal or silver miners, with a strong ancestral tie and schooling in a philosophy of sworn-brotherhood society were akin to Hung's revolutionary ideas. Soon they became the men of Taiping who sparked the revolution in Kuei county which aroused the whole of China to build a heavenly kingdom of brother-hood.

The Hakka were freedom loving and rebellious and they were proud of what they were. The powerful tradition of resistance was par-ticularly their pride. It was their claim that "the regiments which fought against the Mongols were recruited from among them; that the men who followed Coxinga, the loyal Ming general, to Formosa to resist the Manchus, were Hakkas; Hung Hsiu-chuan, as well as many other leaders of the Taiping uprising, were Hakkas."[61] The claim of their ac-tive participation in the Cheng regime might provide one of the pos-sible links to the origins of *kongsi*. The Cheng regime was of course largely a Fukienese sea-merchant kingdom. It is, however, certain that there was a small number of Hakka in the regime, who held official

---

59. *Tai-ping T'ien-kuo Chi-yi T'iao-cha Pao-kao* (Report of the finding of Taiping), (Peking, 1956) p.107.
   Lo, *K'o Chia*, p.417.
60. *Tai-ping*, p.107.
61. Han Suyin, pp.27,28.

positions. One third of the Taiwan population was the Hakka. Their migration began during the time of the Cheng regime.[62] Waves of Hakka migration to Taiwan of this period and later brought the knowledge of Fukien *kongsi* to their home countries and overseas.

And now, the Hakka, with their passion for adventure, mining and brotherhood, had come to break the silence of the mountains in West Borneo.

---

62. Lo, *K'o chia*, pp.12,13.

Chapter 4

THE BORNEO 'FRONTIER' AND THE BEGINNING OF CHINESE SELF-GOVERNMENT

1. The 'Free Frontier' in West Borneo

Most writers disagree regarding the exact year in which Chinese gold mining in the area began. But they all agree that Chinese miners were first introduced by the Panemban of Mampawa. In about 1760, according to Veth, the Panemban who e very possible learnt of the success of the Bangka Sultan in making a great fortune from Chinese tin mining there, invited 20 Chinese from Brunei to dig gold in the Doeri valley. "The result was tremendous," said Veth, "As a result, not only more Chinese were allowed by him to work gold-fields in his kingdom, but also the Sultan of Sampas, Omar Akamadin, was happy to follow his example by permitting the Chinese to establish a mining settlement in Larah around 1760."[1]

This date must have been a mistake, because the grave of a Chinese miner near Montrado has been dated back to the 1740s.[2] This evidence suggested that the beginning of Chinese gold mining in West Borneo was most likely in the 1740s. Veth and Schaannk differ in their accounts of how the Chinese gold miners spread in the pioneering period. The diffusion of early Chinese gold mines, according to Veth, was from Larah to Montrado. But Schaannk believes that Seminis was the point of origin for Chinese gold mines in West Borneo.[3]

The policy of the Malay rulers to encourage Chinese gold mining proved more than successful. At the outset, it was only a trickle of Chinese miners from Brunei, not more than 20 persons. But as soon as

---

1.   Veth, Vol.1, p.298.
2.   Schaannk, p.506.
3.   Schaannk, p.507.

words went round along junk routes to China that rich gold mines were discovered in West Borneo and Chinese miners were welcome, it turned into a flood. As a result of a growing influx of Chinese miners, by 1764 there were 12 mining unions in Larah and 24 in Montrado.[4] The Chinese population underwent a rapid growth. At this time, each year at least 3000 Chinese arrived from China, whereas only few a hundred returned.[5] More Chinese meant more income for the Malay chiefs who seemed little worried about the Chinese. They appeared unable to foresee that what they were doing was inviting a power which they would be in no condition to control in the future.[6]

Since they would rather leave the Chinese alone in their own mining districts, they were not interested in ruling the Chinese politically. It was economic control which concerned them most. They granted mining rights to the Chinese on strict conditions, which were essentially a form of economic control over the Chinese. The Chinese were not allowed to engage in agriculture nor the whole-sale trade, so that they had to rely entirely on the Sultan for their supply of provisions. The compulsory supply of provisions such as rice, iron tools, opium, blue linen and so on was often at highly inflated prices. Also, an annual tribute of 32,000 guilders had to be sent to the Sultan.[7]

All such measures of economic 'control' were aiming to put Chinese miners in a position of permanent economic dependence on the Sultan in order to ensure a lion's share for him in the expanding mining economy. Yet the success of such an economic policy depended on Chinese obedience. Fears of Chinese resistance to such 'control' caused the Sultan to prohibit the Chinese to have firearms and gunpowder. For the same reason, the Sultan was said to have appointed Dayak chiefs to supervise or even exercise authority over the Chinese.[8] This, however desirable from the point of view of the Sultans, seems doubtful in the light of an account given by the Larah Dayaks. That

---

4.   Veth, Vol.1, p.299.
5.   J.H. Moor, *Notice of the Indian Archipelago*, (Singapore, 1837) p.9.
6.   Veth, Vol.1, p.297.
7.   Veth, Vol.1, p.300.
8.   Veth, Vol.1, p.300.

Dayaks was massacred by the Chinese in an insurrection in 1770 as retold by Schaannk, Veth, and De Rees, is even more doubtful.

Veth's version is much less biased than De Ree's against the Chinese. In his account, the Chinese resented the prohibitions even during the reign of Sultan Akamadin, who already found it difficult to uphold economic control. After 10 years of paying tribute reluctantly, the Chinese felt themselves already strong enough to get rid of this yoke. Their first move was to remove the Dayaks' supervision over them. So the story goes:

> On the occasion of their annual feast, the Chinese invited neighbouring Dayaks from Montrado to come over for the celebration. The Dayaks were allowed to enter their fortification (which I think was the *kongsi*-house), only one by one. The Chinese had already armed themselves with weapons. All of a sudden, when the entrance was closed, they made a bloodbath upon the unsuspecting Dayaks. The remaining Dayaks barely escaped the murderous Chinese by fleeing to Bintanan. It happened around 1770 and since then the tribute to the Sultan of Sambas decreased considerably and was collected with difficulty.[9]

The Bangka experience leads me to cast doubt on this account. If the policy of encouraging Chinese gold mining was a leaf taken out of the Bangka Sultan's book, the Malay chiefs in West Borneo must have also learnt about the *kongsi* system there. The Malay *tikus* or treasurers in the court practically left the administration of the mines to the *kongsi* which acted as its agents.[10] The *kongsi* there, being the representatives of the court of Palembang, exercised absolute power over the miners, including their lives and properties. The *kongsi* were themselves Chinese. Even with this form of indirect rule, there were still instances of revolts of the miners. The miners of Jebus, for instance, "are particularly celebrated on account of their obstinacy and impudence, and they have several times been riotous".[11] There were several outrages of the

---

9. Veth, Vol.1, p.300.
10. Thomas Horsefield, 'View of the Tin mines on Bangka', in J.I.A., 1848, Vol.2, p.820.
11. Thomas, p.820.

miners and Chinese inhabitants in the district of Pangkai-pinang too. If indirect rule through the Chinese was already difficult, then to rule the Chinese through the Dayaks would certainly be almost impossible.

The Larah Dayaks told Schaannk their own version of this period of history. The earliest Chinese gold mining, according to them, started with the Sultan of Sambas who sponsored 7 Chinese from Pinang island to dig gold on his account. These 7 Chinese established a mine in mountain Si Benoewang, halfway between Bangkajang and Sebelauw. They were supplied with rice, dried fish and tools by the Sultan.[12] The issue of provisions was made in advance at so high a price that the miners had to give up a large part of their gain in return. It seems, however, much the same as the system of granting monthly advances of articles to tin miners by the *kongsi* in Bangka. But of course, there was a significant difference in Sambas, where the Sultan monopolized the supply of provisions by himself without an agency of *kongsi*.

The Larah Dayak's source has also told much the same story about the gold rush and the prohibitions imposed upon the Chinese who were to be kept strictly to gold mining. Yet fresh light is shed upon how the situation got out of the Sultan's hands as a result of the peaceful erosion of his power by the Chinese. We learn that [13]

"while the Sultan could see with joy that his income increased, this joy did not last long as gradually the influence of the Chinese began to rise above him. The Chinese made every attempt to liberate themselves from the extortion of the Sultan. They smuggled in their provisions and fraternized with the Dayaks more and more. As a consequence, more and more Dayaks were won over by them and a large part of the Sultan's influence was thus diminished."

The Dayak source had no recollection of Dayaks even being appointed to exercise control over the Chinese, who, in their earlier impression, were the coolies of the Sultan. They only gradually came to know that the Chinese were well disposed towards them.[14]

---

12. Schaannk, p.561.
13. Schaannk, p.563.
14. Schaannk, p.563.

The Chinese ascendancy which the Malay chiefs were unable to arrest seems likely to have been due to the success of their fraternization with the Dayaks rather than a massacre as mentioned above. Moreover, we are also told that the Chinese ascendancy was, if not directly, at least indirectly responsible for the political eclipse of the Sultan. Since then, the Sultan of Sambas found himself losing control over the Dayaks. Encouraged by the example of Chinese resistance, various Dayak tribes in Sambas ceased to wage war on each other and united to resist the compulsory trade which brought profit only to the Malay Sultan.[15]

In general, the relationship between the Chinese and Dayaks was good and amicable. There were, however, times when the two groups were at war and times when the Chinese attacked the Dayaks or the Dayaks attacked the Chinese.[16] The Dayaks living in Chinese districts or territories within the power of the *kongsi* were usually on good terms with the Chinese. They were often through marriage of their relations with the Chinese being invited to Chinese feast and became able to speak Chinese. On the other hand, the Malay Sultans could not profit by the Dayaks other than the compulsory barter with which the Dayaks agreed. In this barter, the Dayaks in spite of excessive high profit advanced by them, they could only get salt and tobacco in return.[17]

Dayaks supervision seems extremely unlikely more especially when the Malays rulers were not interested in extending their administration to the Chinese at all. What they sought after was no other than economic control. The kind of economic control, which was in force at the beginning, was in fact a form of feudal overlordship plus unequal partnership. In this unequal partnership, the Malay chiefs 'employed' the Chinese coolies by supplying provisions and tools. This was possible only when the number of Chinese gold miners was very small, not more than a few hundred people. But when the mining

---

15. Ibid.
16. Yeh's Annuals in Lo, pp.139,142.
17. Veth, Vol.1, p.100.
    Jackson, p.44.

population expanded to tens of thousands in the 1770s, it would be an impossible task for the Malay chiefs to supply the provisions and tools. It was clearly no longer possible for the Sultan to continue the monopoly of provisions. This means that he ceased to be the partner or 'employer' of the Chinese miners. A new form of economic control over the Chinese miners was therefore called for. By the time Hunt visited West Borneo in 1812, the Sultan of Sambas collected tribute and mine rents from the Chinese who nominally recognized him as the feudal overlord and landlord of the mines. The mine rent now was fixed at the rate of 50 bunkals of gold per mine per annum. In addition, a capitation tax of 3 dollars per head on every Chinese miner was collected by him. But even such form of economic control was in doubt. As Hunt observed: "There are thirty thousand Chinese in the Sambas district, and they feel themselves strong enough to oppose or evade this tax; it hence becomes a perpetual contest between greedy extortion on the one side and avaricious chicanery on the other."[18]

We do not hear any more about the monopoly of provisions by the Sultan. Already in the 1770s, the Malay chiefs were unable to enforce their ban on Chinese involvement in agriculture. Beginning from the T'ien-Ti Hui and the Lan-fang Hui which first eluded the ban, the other Chinese unions of *kongsi* all sooner or later stepped into agriculture.[19]

It was after 1770 that the Sultan ceased to be the 'employer' of Chinese miners, although he might still have retained the monopoly of opium. The question of political control did not arise until this time because at first the Sultan recruited Chinese miners as his coolies in a number that was too small to have any political significance. However, the expansion of Chinese mining was at a rate far too rapid and of a size far too big for the Malay chiefs to exert political control. In other words, they were completely unprepared for the emergence of a new political power – the *kongsi* – which was to overshadow them.

18. Hunt, in Moor, Appendix, p.18.
19. Schaannk, p.518.
   To be specific, it should be sometime after the defeat of the T'ien-Ti Hui, which monopolized rice production, in 1775 that the rice production became free to all *kongsi*. See Schaannk, p.520.

Their unpreparedness was not altogether due to a lack of foresight. It had a lot to do with other no less important factors as well. Perhaps, the most important one should be sought in the breach of the *kongsi* system of Bangka by the Malay chiefs in West Borneo. The *kongsi* system in Bangka created a class of Chinese *kongsi* who used the authority of Malay *tikus* to run the administration of mines and to monopolize the supply of provisions and tools. They owed their privileges and power to the Malay rule, in which they clearly had a stake. The *kongsi* system there was still very much in the tradition of the old Kapitan system or the traditional Chinese officer system. The *kongsi*, like the kapitan, were appointed as the heads of the Chinese settlement by the Malay rulers. However, the Malay chiefs in West Borneo, who wanted a larger share of mining profit, refused to share the cake with a class of *kongsi*. They acted as direct 'employers' of Chinese coolies and took the monopoly of provisions completely to themselves. Yet they themselves were unable to fill the administrative function of Chinese *kongsi*.

This breach of the old *kongsi* system left the question of the administration of Chinese mine wide open. What were they to do then? They could not be bothered, and left it to Chinese miners themselves to work out their own administration. The Chinese miners knew very well what to do for themselves. They elected administrators who were called *kongsi* and built their government which was called *kongsi* too. The breach of the old *kongsi* system by the Malay chiefs in this way raised the possibility of the emergence of a new form of *kongsi* or Chinese miner government, in which both the officers and miners united as one person.

2. The Pioneering Period: Small partnership, *Shan-sha* or *Parit*

During the pioneering period, from 1745 to 1763, many small Chinese partnerships mushroomed in the gold-fields of West Borneo. They were, no doubt, the very beginning of the Chinese *kongsi* evolution. Chinese *kongsi* names like *Shih-wu-fen* (fifteen shares) and *Shih-san-fen* (thirteen shares) are evidently a relic of their pioneering past. The tales of first Chinese gold mines in Sambas and Mampawa, all with no more than 20 miners under the Malay sponsorship, also points to their origin in small partnerships.

Whether already the small partnerships were called *kongsi* in this period, we are not certain. However, we are told that they were definitely called *Shan-sha* (the sand of mountain) or *Parit* which in Malay means canal or mine. Lo Fang-po has left us a passage about *parit* in his poem:[20]

> The customs of naming things are so very different here. Seldom can the Chinese and the barbarian communicate. Yet the so-called *Sha-liao* are actually huts for miners, and *parit Chin-hu* (lakes of gold-fields) by different name.

Parit, or *Shan-sha*, according to Francis, generally was referring to a small mine operated by 10 to 25 men who included the cook and handicraft workers.[21] Such small mining operations were invariably organized on the basis of the traditional Chinese partnership system – the *huo-chi* system.[22] So it appears in the oral tradition of the Larah Dayak that the miners were closely bound to each other by a specific tie, by which miners of the same mine regarded one another as comrade or *huo-chi*.

As regards *Shan-sha* in this period, we are almost totally left in the dark. Much of those which we know are of later period. Veth, however, says:[23]

> All these small mines are called *shan-sha* by the Chinese. They were different from the large mines or *Nam* by their insignificant amount of capital, their smaller number of labourers, their simpler structure of organization, and their lack of extensive waterwork, as a result, the water supply of which was very much dependent on the rain and by their exclusive working on the gold-ore which lay closer to the upper layer. In general, the proportion was not unlike that which existed between the kulit- and kollong-mines in tin mining in Bangka.

---

20. Lo, p.148.
21. Francis, p.23.
    Veth. p.333.
22. Schaannk, p.562.
23. Veth, Vol.1, p.334.

Small mines or kulit mines generally suffered such drawbacks as early exhaustion of the ore and often longer stoppage of the works because of the small supply of water.[24] However, the kulit mines on the hill-deposits were suitable for small capital. Although, when possible in this early period, Malay rulers might have been acting in the capacity of suppliers of tools, provisions and opium, similar to *wo-tou* in Yünnan, Chinese miners seemed to have raised capital for their mining operation by themselves. They organized small partnerships not only for raising capital but also for mutual support and help. The shareholders were called *hun* who participated in the loss or gain according to their shares.[25] Every member had had to work in the mine. Meanwhile, "even those who had more than one share still had to take part in the labour, until they employed workers to work for them".[26] Their substitutes were called coolie-hun.[27]

The beginning of Chinese gold mining was started by Malay sponsorship. Later, however, most of the Chinese migrants came to West Borneo without the invitation or sponsorship by the Malay chiefs who of course still welcomed this new source of income. These Chinese small partnerships which did not rely on the Malay chiefs for the supply of tools and capital, grew numerous and extensive over time. They had to pay a certain amount of gold for the right to mine and to put up with the compulsory trade through which the workers were supplied with the provisions at high prices.[28]

Even that small in scale, not more than 25, the *Shan-sha* had its own administration independent of Malay rule. Not unlike the *k'o-chang* system in Yünnan, in the *Shan-sha* or small partnership,[29]

> Every shareholder had a vote in the affairs of the enterprise. A clerk was elected for every four months to run the daily business and to keep the account of incomes and expenses. He was temporarily con-

---

24. Posewitz, p.353.
25. Posewitz, p.359.
26. Veth, Vol.1, p.303.
27. Posewitz, p.359.
28. Veth, Vol.1, p.333.
29. Veth, p.303.

sidered as the head. But as soon as his term of office finished, he must lay down his pen and go out to work with a mattock as an ordinary member.

This clerk might be called *kongsi* or the officer. He was not responsible to Malay rulers but his partnership. The officer of the *parit* was almost indistinguishable from the rest of the partners who elected him as the head only for four months. To them, he was only a partner, who had just as equal a say in the matter of the *parit* as any ordinary member had. In contrast, the Chinese mining officers in Bangka were divorced from the miners and formed a distinctive class of their own. There the Chinese *kongsi* were vested by Malay *tikus* "with authority to regulate everything relating to the mines and to the persons employed by them".[30]

It was so not only because of the concentration of power in the hands of the *kongsi* who built up a machinery of administration by appointing a number of writers, store-keepers and assistants to assist him. Even in economic terms, the Chinese *kongsi* in Bangka were also an exploiting class. It was they who used the fund provided by his employer, the *tikus*, to supply the miners with "the machinery of various kinds used in mining; besides furnaces, apparatus and implements of smelting of the ore".[31] It was also they who by using the same fund supplied the tin miners with monthly advances in rice, salt, oil and clothes of various kinds at high prices.[32]

This contrasts with the position of Chinese officers in West Borneo. They were deprived by the Malay rulers of such an economic function on the one hand, and of such a concentration of political power on the other. These differences, the lack of an instrument of Malay official control and the electoral power of miners over the officers led to a different evolution of Chinese mining partnerships in West Borneo. The evolution of the Chinese *kongsi* in West Borneo was blessed with a good environment for self-government from the begin-

---

30. Thomas Horsefield, p.820.
31. Ibid.
32. Thomas Horsefield, p.820.

ning. This position was not changed until nearly a century later when the Dutch left no room for Chinese autonomy.

The spread and growth of *shan-sha* or small partnerships continued well into a much later period when the large *kongsi* government had already evolved from its *shan-sha* origin. Within the *kongsi*, there were many independent small mining partnerships growing like mushrooms under the shade of a tall tree. Those independent *shan-sha* of Koelor, Sebawa, Seminis and Siding lasted until 1850.[33] The number of them, according to Veth, was rather considerable.[34] These small mines within the *kongsi* were, however, obliged to give part of their profit to the *kongsi* for the grant of the mining right.[35]

Before the emergence of Chinese mining brotherhood government in 1763, the gold rush in West Borneo caused a sudden multiplication of small mining partnerships. Numerous *stamgenoten* or family or clan partnerships arose from both the Chinese who wrote asking their clan members to come over and the newcomers who looked for their relatives and clan members.[36] According to Schaannk, these clan partnerships were ruled by patriarchal government, in which the eldest and most venerable were naturally the unchosen heads.[37]

This, in fact, was the *k'o-chang* system of traditional private Chinese mining, being mistaken by Schaannk for patriarchal government.[38] Hsieh Ching-kao a widely travelled sea-merchant from Chiaying Chou, who also had been to the West Borneo, wrote in 1842:[39]

From Kuta to Wanlah, mountains linked together. People travelled by land. In the district of Mondor, tens of thousands of the Chinese from Canton and Fukien were gold miners, farmers and traders. In countries of Tai-yen, Yi-hao, Hsin-tan there were also a few hundred Chinese in each place. They were free to move about regardless of

33. Veth, Vol.1. p.334.
    Jackson, pp.63,64.
34. Veth, Vol.1, p.333.
35. Veth, Vol.1, p.333.
36. Schaannk, p.564.
37. Schaannk, p.565.
38. In order to refresh the memory, see Chapter.1, the section on the *k'o-chang* system.
39. Lo, p.134.

boundaries between them. It was all depending on where would they live that year that they paid the capitation tax collected by the *k'o-chang* of the place to the Dutch.

Hsü Chi-yü too identified the Chinese *kongsi* administrators as the *k'o-chang*. Without making it clear when it was, he wrote in 1850:[40]

> In recent years, the Chinese from Chia-ying chou went into interior mountains to open up mines. More and more Chinese migrants settled down and became naturalized. They at first married with the Dayak women. When the population greatly multiplied after generations, they began to marry with the growing number of native born Chinese women. The population now has already exceeded twenty or thirty thousand. They selected the elders for the administration of the *kongsi* whom they called by the name of *k'o-chang*. In every one or two years, the officers were replaced.

It is apparent in this description that the system was one in which the elders ranked high and venerable but also one that was for the small and simple organization. So, I think they must be talking about the pioneering period although they themselves might not be aware of the confusion of time caused by their discursiveness. The head of the small partnership or *parit* who was elected to run the daily business of the *parit* for four months must have held the title *k'o-chang* or *k'o-t'ou*. This tradition passed down well into a much later time when the large *kongsi* federation incorporated both the *kongsi-parit* and small private partnerships which were independent. As opposed to the *kongsi-parit* that belonged to the *kongsi*, the small private partnership were still called *k'o-tou-parit*.[41]

---

40. Wei Yuan, *Hai-kuo t'u-chih*, chuan 12, Hai-tao-kuo 2, p.5.
41. Schaannk, p.568.

Chapter 5

THE RISE OF BROTHERHOOD GOVERNMENT AND *KONGSI* GOVERNMENTS

1. The rise of brotherhood government – *Hui*

In 1763 or thereabouts, there was a further development of Chinese miner organizations. *Hui* – a form of miner brotherhood government emerged from the combination of small partnerships. *Hui*, in Chinese, means union, which in itself, of course, does not imply the largeness or smallness of the organization. Nevertheless, something in the nature of brotherhood government is being introduced by this new usage of the old term.

The birth of Chinese mining *hui* was partly the result of organizational reform and expansion. Indeed, the rapidly expanding mining economy during the pioneering period encouraged the growth of larger mining operations and organizations. There were far greater advantages in organizational reform. In order to be better able to deal with the Dayaks and rapacious Malay rulers, and to have more human resources for large-scale mine work such as water networks, small partnerships began to unite into one single union of *hui* brotherhood.[1]

Although in general a mining *hui* brotherhood embraced 50 to 150 members,[2] twice or thrice as big as the *shan-sha* in 1763, many of the 24 mining *hui* in Montrado were small, perhaps no bigger than small partnerships. However, those which were of greater means, labour and capital as well, built the large mines on the relatively flat valley plains where deposits were often thicker and deeper. This kind of large mine,

1. Schaannk, p.565.
2. Francis, p.23.
3. Jackson is right to link the emergence of the *Nam* with the growth of Chinese self-government. But its appearance was not towards the end of the nineteenth century but much earlier. See Jackson, p.38.

which was called *nam*, never needed to stop work for want of water. It, furthermore, gave longer yield of the ore than the *shan-sha*.[3]

During the emergence of mining brotherhoods, violence erupted over conflicting claims to the mining rights by contending *hui*. Almost as a rule, the expansion of a mining brotherhood also meant the expansion of the mining territory, even at the cost of the other mining *hui*. Thus, gradually in a specific district only one brotherhood arose as the strongest who laid claim to the whole area of neighbourhood and more or less obtained the marked out territory.[4] In the Chinese districts, the small partnerships, as Veth observed, regarded themselves the exclusive owners of the gold mines. As soon as the news that a gold mine was discovered, was reported to the *kongsi* or brotherhood, they hurried off to occupy the mine and to apply for the *kongsi's* approval of their mining rights over the new mine.[5] Within the territory of a *kongsi*,[6]

> He who has neglected to report the discovery of a new gold-field to the *kongsi* whose territory their kampong or dessa belonged to, and he who takes the risk of being on his own authority to dig for gold in the new mine, be he a Chinese, Malay or Dayak will be penalized · with a heavy fine and sometimes with horrible mutilation.

While more and more mining *hui* were expanding their territories, and therefore their members, the number of small partnerships standing by themselves certainly progressively dwindled. The small partnerships which had yet to join a *hui* brotherhood, would be persuaded by their own interest to do so. Even those which appeared more or less independent still had to rely upon their alliance with one or another *hui* brotherhood for protection.[7] By 1774, after the defeat of the Lan-fang *hui*, the number of mining *hui* in Montrado was reduced from 24 to 12, which 3 years later had merged into 7.[8] The exact number was, however, debatable. Schaannk strongly argued that it was 14

4. Schaannk, p.565.
5. Veth, Vol.1, p.333.
6. Ibid.
7. Schaannk, p.565.
8. eth, Vol.1, pp.299,301.

rather than 12 after 1774. He nevertheless admitted of the possibility of the existence of 12 mining *hui* in Montrado before 1772.[9]

The reason for this is that not all the new mining *hui* were formed by the unification of the old partnerships. Some new mining *hui* were split from the old partnerships which had grown too big to remain one. Hsin-pa-fen (the new eight shares) for instance, was split from the Lao-pa-fen (old eight shares). Similarly, the Hsin-shih-ssu-fen (the new fourteen shares) stemmed from the pa-fen (the eight shares) and shih-ssu-fen (the fourteen shares). The Lao-shih-ssu-fen (the old fourteen shares) was also the mother *kongsi* or *hui* of the Hsin-wuk (the new house).[10]

The process of merging pursued no definite pattern. An element of clannism was discernible in the organization of *hui* brotherhoods. Ta-kang (the great port) which emerged as the largest and strongest *kongsi* later, consisted, for the most part, of the surname groups of Wu, Huang and Cheng from Hui-lai and Lu-feng. A large part of Shan-t'iao-kuo (the three ditches) likewise comprised the surname groups of Weng and Chu also from Hui-lai and Lu-feng. In Lan-fang (the orchard-fragrance) big surname groups of Sung, Liu and Chiang from Chia-ying chou formed the majority.

Clannism in this early stage of the *kongsi's* evolution was, however, not so strong as in the 1840s. The old and narrow concept of *hui* brotherhood based on regionalism or clannism was necessarily modified and enlarged by the expansion of Chinese mining organizations in West Borneo. The founding of the Lan-fang *hui* was such an extension of the *hui* brotherhood. Although the nucleus of the Lan-fang brotherhood was no doubt formed by over a hundred Chia-ying Hakka, its growth was the continued extension of the brotherhood to the miners from other regions. Soon after their takeover the *Shan-shin* (the heart of the mountain) mine, they treated the Ta-p'u Hakka there as their brother.[11] Many other of the same group, whether called Ta-p'u Hakka or Chao-young Hakka or Chao-chou Hakka must also have

9. Schaannk, pp.522,523.
10. Schaannk, pp.523,524.
11. Lo, p.138.

been thereafter embraced into this enlarged brotherhood in much the same way.

Mining unions during this period were simultaneously called *hui* and *kongsi*. Both Schaannk and Veth have pointed out that initially, Chinese mining unions in West Borneo had been called *hui*.[12] Yeh's *Annals*, which also confirm this, say that Lo Fang-po, the legendary founder of Lan-fang, was highly regarded by the *Shih-ta Chia-wui* (the four big families) and the *Ch'i-sheng kongsi* (the accumulation of victories) when he first arrived in Pontianak.[13] The simultaneous usage of the terms *kongsi* and *hui* by the Chinese mining unions in West Borneo may sound confusing to us nowadays. But to the men of *kongsi* or *hui*, it was only a matter of different emphasis.

When they placed the emphasis on the meaning of brotherhood they used the term *hui*. But when they tried to distinguish their organizations from the *hui* brotherhoods in China, and to stress the significance of the extended partnership, they created a new usage for the old term *kongsi*. For, unlike *hui* brotherhoods in general in China, theirs were at once extended mining partnerships and brotherhoods, the unity of which was symbolized in a Hall or *kongsi* house. Yeh's *Annals* tell a tale of the Lan-fang *kongsi's* evolution from the foundation of the Central Hall or *kongsi* house:[14]

> After the occupation of *Shan-shin* gold mine, Lo Fang-po erected stockades and walls around the houses there. He was conceiving a plan of gradual expansion to neighbouring areas. Since then his reputation and influence grew daily. As he became a force to be reckoned with in the region, people from all over the region came to join him. They consequently founded the *tsung-t'ing* or the Central Hall of the Lan-fang *kongsi* at Mondor. With an increasing number of resident houses and shops built in the vicinity of the Central Hall, a thriving township thereby emerged from the mine.

This version is, of course, somewhat idealized. The expansion of the Lan-fang brotherhood had, for the most part, not been peaceful.

---

12. Veth, Vol.1, p.330.
13. Lo, p.137.
14. Lo, p.138.

Mao-ern, a prospering mining settlement comprising more than 200 shops, was added to its territory by a surprise attack with the collaboration of the Chia-ying Hakka from within. Its military campaigns for the expansion of territory were not at all smooth sailing. The war with powerful brotherhood of Liu Chien-hsian had been going on with ups and downs for years. At one point the Lan-fang *hui* was even in great danger of being wiped out by the joined forces of Liu's brotherhood and other mining camps from Ming Huang to Liu fen-t'ou.[15] The enemy forces were only a few hundred yards away. However, the scale of war finally turned by a boost of morale on Lo's side. In the decisive battle, Lo personally fought in the front line and broke Liu's six military camps and his allied forces with a single stroke. The victory not only recovered his loss in land but also put the entire Mondor region under his control.[16]

Chinese mining *hui* have mistakenly been regarded by Schaannk as a form of patriarchal government. They, indeed, were nothing but brotherhood governments. Their organization as described by Yeh's *Annals* was as follows:[17]

> The mining settlement of Mao-ern was just prospering. There were two towns, the Oldtown and the Newtown. Oldtown was estimated to have had more than 200 shops and Newtown more than 20. The Hakka from Chao-yang, Chieh-yang, Hai-feng and Lu-feng, had a majority in Oldtown. Huang Kui-po was elected as the head or the tsung-ta-ko. The Chia-ying Hakka which fashioned the overwhelming majority in Newtown were led by Chiang Mao-po who held the title *kung-yeh*. They formed *Lan-ho ying* (Orchid-Harmony Camp). Four assistant heads called *Lao-man* (elder assistant) were elected to help him.

A brotherhood like this was governed by a five-man administration which seemed small indeed. We do not know how large the membership was. However, the number could be somewhere around two to

---

15. Liu fen-t'ou was a very old mining brotherhood which was the mother-*hui* of Shih-wu-fen (the fifteen shares) to which it later belonged. See Schaannk, p.526.
16. Lo, p.138.
17. Ibid.

three hundred people by inference from the fact that there were no more than 20 shops in Newtown. The organization was in part inspired by a heritage of their forefathers who had created the Eternal Prosperity Brotherhood a century earlier in Hui-chou. The prototype had been a much larger organization but nevertheless had a five-man administration at the highest level. The fifth leader too, had borne the title *Man-tsung* or *Wui-tsung*, both of which meant assistant head.

Almost invariably all presidents of Chinese mining brotherhoods in West Borneo carried the title *po*. The title holders included presidents of different *hui*, for example, Chiang Mao-po, Huang Kui-po, Lo Fang-po and Hsieh Chieh-po. The succeeding presidents of the same brotherhood or *kongsi* were also honoured with the title by using it as their last names, a name habit which was uniquely Chinese, and clearly associated with the rise of a social group to distinction. Similarly, during the sixteenth and seventeenth centuries, Chinese sea captains used the title *kuan* as their last names, to distinguish their rank.[18]

The new title *po* was recognized by Malays as equivalent to Kapitan.[19] The recognition represented a new and significant change from original Malay-Chinese relationship in this period of growing Chinese autonomy, and perhaps, independence, based upon the rise of Chinese mining brotherhoods. Though the title kapitan was old, the recognition that a Kapitan or President of a Chinese brotherhood exercised absolute authority in its own territory was certainly new. One of such recognitions was well documented in the appointment of Kapitan Bapah Wu or Wu Yüan-sheng, by the Panembahan of Mampawa as the absolute authority in Sinaman in 1770:[20]

> The Panembahan has entrusted to Kapitan Bapah Wu all their affairs of Sinaman and the administration of justice. Whatever public announcements and command that would be made, they shall be made by Kapitan Bapah Wu and nobody else. For good or bad, it would

---

18. See Chen Ching-ho, 'Ching-chu Hua-po chi Chang-chi Mao-I' (The Role of Chinese Junks in Nagasaki-South China Trade and Navigation during Early Ch'ing) in JSSS. Vol.9, Part 1, pp.15-50.
19. Schaannk, p.586.
20. Schaannk, p.586.

rest with Kapitan Bapah Wu. Anybody who disobeys the order or command of Kapitan Bapah Wu, will be considered just as much an offense to the Panembahan. If his offense is so grave that he should be put to death, he will be executed, or that he deserves punishment, then he will be punished, be he a Bugis, Malay, or Dayak or Chinese.

The Malay official recognition of Kapitan's power as such departed sharply from the traditional Kapitan system in which the Chinese kapitan was appointed to rule the Chinese community only. Wu's brotherhood, however, must have established its complete control over all races in the territory of Sinaman before the Malay official recognition of its power as an accomplished fact. One after another Chinese mining brotherhoods likewise fell away from Malay and Dayaks who lived within their territories. It was from this point on that a new form of political power, the Chinese mining brotherhood or *kongsi* had become dominant in West Borneo.

The origin of the term *po* was, no doubt, with the great founders who had been the first to found a Chinese settlement or brotherhood, especially those of the Hakka. De Groot is correct in pointing out that the founder was the *Ta-po-kung* or the patron-god of the *kongsi* and that for this reason, the founder of the Lan-fang *kongsi* had been recognized as Lo Ta-po or Lo Po-kung.[21] Many other great founders of Chinese-mining brotherhoods in West Borneo had also been honoured with this term. Liu Shan-po, the formidable founder of the T'ien-ti brotherhood, was one, and Hsieh Chieh-po, the founder of the Ho-shun *kongsi* federation, the other.[22]

---

21. De Groot, p.120,121.
22. Schaannk, p.520.

> *Ta-po-kung* had been a Chinese deification of great mariners in origin. It had been variably called *Tu-kung* in the Ming and *Nu-kung* from the end of the Ming to the middle of the Ch'ing. But since then it evolved into the enshrined memory of the great founders of Chinese settlements overseas. The earliest temple of *Ta-po-kung* in Pinang was built to deify a Hakka founder with the surname Chang. The men of the *kongsi* in West Borneo similarly honoured the founders of *kongsis* with deification. Although Lo Hsiang-lin insists of *Ta-po-kung* being only the *Tu-ti* (earth god), my agreement is with Purcell's evolutionary image of *Ta-po-kung*, which is more historical.

In 1776, the Hsieh Presidency of the Ho-shun *kongsi* federation was interestingly associated with a union of the titles kapitan and *po* in his name, Hsieh Chieh-chia and Hsieh Chieh-po. At this juncture the men of the *kongsi* had already created a more developed framework of organization for the greater union of Chinese mining brotherhoods.

2. The Construction of an extended brotherhood – *kongsi* Government

Significant changes occurred in the 1770s when Chinese mining brotherhoods moved speedily towards a greater union. By this time, most of the mining *kongsi* already had large membership by comparison. While during the period of small partnership, often a partnership had twenty to fifty members, in the times of brotherhood, a brotherhood generally consisted of one hundred to two hundred men. Now, in 1774, a *kongsi* usually comprised five to six hundred members. We are told that Ta-kang at this stage had a membership of five to six hundred, and Chieh-lian (the Link), Shan-t'iao-kuo (the Three Ditches), Hsin-pa-fen (the New Eight Shares) and Hsin-wuk (the New House) each about eight hundred.[23]

This general trend of enlarging mining organization in Montrado at least, was partly intensified by a common fear of the Heaven and Earth Brotherhood amongst the smaller brotherhoods. After the defeat of the Lan-fang *hui*, the Heaven and Earth Brotherhood had become the big bully of Montrado. This fear was said to have set in motion a process of incorporation and alliance amongst smaller brotherhoods. The miners who saw much interest in extending their brotherhoods

---

In the portrayal of Purcell, *Ta-po-kung* is linked with the history of overseas Chinese: "He probably derives from Tu Ti, but overseas he is primarily the spirit of the pioneers. The Chinese pioneers of the early days suffered terrible hardships and were honoured in memory by those who came after them. Toh Peh Kong seems to be the personification of the pioneer spirit generally and is not the deification of a special person as Sam Po Tai Shan is of Cheng Ho." See Han Wai-toon, *Ta-po-kung-kao* (Research on *Ta-po-kung*) in JSSS, Vol.1, part.2.

Kuang Kuo-hsiang, *Ping-lang-I Hai-chou-I Ta-po-kung* (Notes on *Ta-po-kung* in Tanjong Tokong, Penang) in JSSS, Vol. 9, Part 1. Lo, p.89.

Purcell, p.49.

23. Schaannk, p.520.

into a larger organization formed, therefore, *kongsi*. As a result, the number of small brotherhoods grew fewer and fewer until there were only fourteen *kongsi* in Montrado in 1774.

The Heaven and Earth Brotherhood which probably had a membership of five to six hundred had been imposing a monopoly policy of rice and other items upon other mining brotherhoods. In 1775, not only was rice sold at high prices but also sugar-cane. In particular, sugar from the gardens of Rantouw was now and then not allowed in. Its members even grew so aggressive to take liberties with the women of other *kongsi* and to plunder other *kongsi* of their properties. All these abuses and the oppression on the part of the Heaven and Earth Brotherhood certainly threw it into a violent collision with the fourteen other *kongsi* which allied together. The alliance of the fourteen *kongsi* must have been ten times stronger than the Heaven and Earth Brotherhood in terms of their memberships and strength. They finally defeated and killed Liu Shan-po and some of his five hundred sworn-brothers. The remainder of the Brotherhood were absorbed into the memberships of the allied *kongsi*.[24]

In 1776, the temporary alliance of the fourteen *kongsi* developed into a *kongsi* federation of permanent nature. The federation was Ho-shun *kongsi* which, in Chinese, means the federation of great peace and harmony, and which embodied a fuller development of extended brotherhood and partnership. The membership the Ho-shun federation in Montrado included the fourteen mining *kongsi* as follows:[25]

1. Ta-kang (the great port)
2. Lao-pa-fen (the old eight shares)
3. Chiu-fen-t'ou (the nine shares)
4. Shih-san-fen (the thirteen shares)
5. Chieh-lien (the link)
6. Hsin-pa-fen (the new eight shares)
7. Shan-t'iao-kou (the three ditches)

---

24. Schaannk, p.520.
25. Based on Schaannk, Jackson draws a map of the geographical locations of the fourteen *kongsi*. Jackson, p.55. See also Appendix I.

8. Man-ho (the perfect peace)
9. Hsin-wuk (the new house)
10. Ker n-wui (the gold-pit's end)
11. Shih-wu-fen (the fifteen shares)
12. Tai-ho (the peace and harmony)
13. Lao-shih-ssu-fen (the old fourteen shares)

The federation, by inferring from the average membership of five to six hundred in each *kongsi*, must have embraced eight to ten thousand Chinese of varied district origins and occupations. The first President of the *Ho-shun* federation was Hsieh Chi-chia. During his presidency, Shan-t'iao-kuo, Chieh-lien, Hsin-pa-fen (the New Eight Shares), Hsin-wuk (the New House) and Ta-kang had had the greatest influence at first. But later only three *kongsi* (the three ditches), Ta-kang, Shan-t'iao-kuo and Chieh-lien were the foremost while there was still a closer tie between Ta-kang and Shan-t'iao-kuo.[26]

The birth of the *Ho-shun* federation brought a period of great expansion to Chinese mining in Montrado. Many new mines were opened. Meanwhile, the Chinese *kongsi* in Larah had also now established a closer tie with those in Montrado for protection. Just by invoking the name of the *Ho-shun*, the Malays and Dayaks could easily be awe-stricken.[27]

There had been a similar trend of the *kongsi* in Larah towards a greater union. In 1776, the trend had already reduced the number of *kongsi* from the twelve of 1763 to no more than seven in total, comprising:[28]

1. Yüan-ho (the first union)
2. Ying-ho (the amicable union)
3. Chan-ho (the support for union)
4. Hui-ho (the beneficial union)
5. Sheng-ho (the rising union)
6. Shuang-ho (the double harmony)

---

26. Schaannk, p.527.
27. Schaannk, p.527.
28. Ibid.

7.   Hsia-wuk (the lower house)

All of them came under the umbrella of the leading *kongsi* in Montrado. Hui-ho was protected by Chieh-lien. Yüan-ho, Chan-ho and Ying-ho were led by Ta-kang. Sheng-ho and Shuang-ho entered into an alliance with Shan-t'iao-kuo. Hsia-wuk was even called small San-t'iao-kuo because of the close relationship between them. Despite their alliance with the Montrado *kongsi*, they remained in all aspects independent and free to accept new members of their own.[29]

Every founding *kongsi* of the Federation in Montrado had been called *Kai-hsian kongsi*. Each one of them consisted of one or more *kongsi* mines (also called *kongsi*) as well as of private farmers, traders, handicraft workers and miners. Some time, their private miners again formed large mines which also bore the name *kongsi*. Of such, the famous ones were:[30]

1.   Chin-ho (the gold union)
2.   Ta-sheng (the great prosperity)
3.   Kuan-ho (the wide union)
4.   Liu-fen-t'ou (the six shares)
5.   Pa-fen-t'ou (the eight shares)
6.   Chan-ho (the support of union)

Before, during and after the formation of the Federation, the distinction between a *kongsi* and a small private partnership was that a *kongsi* was an enlargement of brotherhood founded within a Chinese settlement and the temple of the *Ta-po-kung*.

Kongsi mines or *kongsi-parit* were operated to bring benefit and profit to the whole union of the enlarged brotherhood which was called *kongsi*. The profit was partly to meet general expenses of the *kongsi*. But although the private mines or *k'o-t'ou-parit* had to pay mine rent to the *kongsi*, they were, in contrast, operated to the undertakers' own benefit. The new members or *Hsin-k'o* usually worked in the *kongsi* mines first, which provided them with food and clothing and a pay of 4

29.   Schaannk, p.528.
30.   Schaannk, p.526.

reaal or 16 florins every four months. The old members or *Lao-k'o* were obliged to take care of the mines. The *kongsi* mine was established by those who parted with their own money to contribute to the fund. The shareholder each had a share of profit and a vote in the election of the heads of the mine.[31]

It is clear that *kongsi* mines were not privately owned. Crawfurd's picture that they were worked by companies of persons of property and capital, who employed monthly labourers, is therefore misleading.[32] This is to transplant a westerner's view of capitalism to a Chinese communal enterprise which had distant roots in China. However, despite this note of scepticism, the following information from him is valuable:[33]

> The mode of paying the labourers is by monthly wages, with a supply of food. An inexperienced labourer receives for the first four months two Spanish dollars, a month, for the second four months, four dollars, and for the remainder of the year five. Even afterwards he received six, and if he has capacity and integrity to make an overseer, eight dollars.

They were paid by the *kongsi* with fixed wages and the supply of food and clothing and accommodation. But for those who worked in small partnerships on their own, they only shared in the gain and loss on terms of perfect equality.

In marked contrast to private partnerships, in every *kongsi* there was a *kongsi*-house or *t'ing*. The *kongsi*-house served as the stockade to fortify the mine, as the temple of their *Ta-po-kung*, as the storehouse of their weapons, tools, provisions, gold and money, as the sleeping quarters of officers and part of their workforce.[34] Its significance in the life of *kongsi* as an institution cannot be overstressed. Indeed, it "was a visible manifestation of the whole *kongsi* system".[35] But most of all, it

---

31. Schaannk, p.568
32. Crawfurd, p.474.
33. Crawfurd, p.475.
34. Schaannk, p.563.
    Jackson, p.69.
35. Jackson, p.70.

was the embodiment of the whole *kongsi* or extended brotherhood. Often, general meetings in the *kongsi*-house had the last say in matters of great importance.

Kongsi membership was open, but it required a fee of 4 florins from anyone who chose to join. The admission fee was called *hui-ti* (the foundation of brotherhood) or *hui-hsin* (the heart of brotherhood).[36] In addition, every new member contributed half a florin to pay for the person who conducted the oath-taking ceremony which was to orientate new members to the brotherhood.[37] The symbolism of the extended brotherhood found full expression in the worship of the *Ta-po-kung*, to whom every new member vowed his loyalty. However, in a manner characteristic of the Chinese, the men of the *kongsi* even symbolized the *kongsi* way of life as *kongsi* rice in the catechism of initiation rituals:[38]

Do you know it is not at all easy to eat *kongsi* rice?
If all the other brothers can, I certainly will.

Then, the oath of allegiance.

The heads of brotherhood were extended to a wide range of Chinese in West Borneo. Almost all the Chinese belonged to one or another brotherhood there were, farmers and handicraft workers in the neighbourhood of mines, traders and fishermen in the coastal kampongs, even the Chinese lived in the midst of a Malay population in the capitals.[39] All of them had been united as well as divided by the ever enlarging brotherhoods which grew increasingly larger but fewer and which were called *kongsi*. The whole Chinese population in West Borneo was an extension of Chinese *kongsi* or brotherhoods.

Every *kongsi* had its own administration filled by the officers who again were also called *kongsi*. The officers varied in number according to the sizes of *kongsi* mines. *Kongsi* officers were all elected by members through a general meeting held in the *kongsi*-house, the seat of

---

36. Schaannk, p.585.
37. Ibid.
38. Ibid.
39. Veth, Vol.1, p.311. Jackson, pp.68,69.

kongsi government. The administration consisted of two or more clerks called *djoeroe-toelis* or *ts'ai-ku* who managed activities of a day to day nature and finance. One or more overseers called *ma'lim* or *huochang* were entrusted with the instruction of the mine labour and the collection of the gold-dust. Experience and honesty were required of him by the *kongsi*-mine workers.[40]

The tenure of office had usually been four months. Once their term of office had expired, they had to return to the rank of ordinary mine workers although they were still eligible for re-election. If they caused discontent in the ranks, the administrators could be dismissed by them anytime through a general meeting. And those who were elected were obliged to accept the office.[41] The leadership was established on a consideration of the substance and ability represented by the leaders. Age and venerability did not count much.[42]

All the *kongsi* officers, except the honorary title holders, were housed, clothed, paid and provided meals by the *kongsi* fund. It had been a very significant institution of the *kongsi* establishment that the *kongsi* officers must live with the *kongsi*-mine workers in the *kongsi*-house. They not only lived under the same roof with the coolies but also ate at the same mat with them. This social equality of the life of the *kongsi* impressed Earl profoundly:[43]

> There appeared to be very little distinction of rank among the people, for the Chinese kulis who carried my baggage, sat down to eat at the same mat with the governor, and frequently dipped their chopsticks into the same dish; this functionary, however, always occupied the upper end. The women joined in the meal, but they were chiefly employed in attending to the wants of the male portion of the company.

A treasurer drew 16 florins a month and an overseer 32 florins. The Kapitan himself received as many as 40 florins or more a month.[44]

40. Veth, Vol.1, p.319. Schaannk, p.571.
41. Veth, Vol.1, p.319. Schaannk, p.575.
42. Schaannk, p.569.
43. Earl, pp.291,293.
44. Earl, pp.291,293.

Their pay as well as the expenses of the *kongsi*-house were met by a *kongsi* fund built up from the profits of the *kongsi* mines. However, the large *kongsi* levied a capitation tax of one or two florins to add to the *kongsi* fund for the general expenses of the *kongsi*.[45] The *kongsi* fund was spent on the salaries of officers, the reception of guests, the celebration of festivals and the expenses of war and so on.

Over the agricultural population in the *kongsi*, the administration was extended through the elders, the *kongsi* wine distillery heads, and the temple heads. The venerable elders were the relics of the old partnerships which formed the *kongsi*. They derived their command of respect and authority not from election but from their age. But during the later period, the *kongsi* leadership was little interfered with by their dwindling influence.[46] The *kongsi* wine distillery heads or *Chiu-lang* were charged with the collection of the *kongsi* taxes. The main responsibility of the temple heads was conducting festivals and controlling commercial funds. Both *Chiu-lang* and *Fu-shou* (the temple heads) shared with the venerable elders the authority in small matters and day to day administration.[47] They all seemed to have derived their pay from their own jobs and not from the *kongsi* fund.

When the *kongsi* went to war, the officers had to go down to become coolies, and they resumed their office only after the war was over. The war effort was commanded by two elected military advisers called *Chun-shi*. Under the *Chun-shi*, field forts commanders called *cha-chu* again were appointed to take charge of the defence of the field-forts as well as the collection of import duties. In normal time, no garrison was stationed in the field-forts. Only a couple of sentries were posted there and in case of danger, the neighbouring town inhabitants, farmers and workers were immediately called up for defence.[48]

---

45. Veth, Vol.1, p.321.
46. Schaannk, p.575.
47. Schaannk, p.576.
48. Schaank, p.576.
49. Schaannk, p.577. Veth says that the *Petompang* or mixed blood Chinese by Dayak mothers were usually the front line fighters. This, however, must have only happened in a later period. Veth, Vol.1, p.323.

In wartime, the workers of the *kongsi* mines were, as a rule, the first to take to the field.[49] Ta-kang, for example, always had about 3,000 fighting men under command in its later period. Everyone in the *kongsi*, however, was obliged to take up arms, not just the *kongsi* miners. The fighting men were paid and fed in wartime by the *kongsi* out of the *kongsi* fund. Prizes of enemy heads were offered to boost ·their morale, two taels of gold for the head of a leader in the enemy camp, 4 florins for that of a Malay, 2 florins for that of a Dayak. However, the capturer of a Dayak women had to give her away to the *kongsi*. He received in return half of her dowry, when she was married by the *kongsi* later.

The normal life of the *kongsi* also stood still under wartime regulations. Not only the mine work was stopped, there was no business as usual: no pig slaughtered, no wine distilled, so that everyone else shared the hardship of war with those who were fighting in the battlefields.[50] War breathed more austerity into the life in *kongsi* than usual.

In Mondor, federalism also triumphed. Only a year later than the Ho-shun federation, the Lan-fang federation emerged there. The federation was formed under the leadership of Lo Fang-po who united Mao-er n, Chu-ta-ya, Kun-jih, Lung-kang and Salaman, either through military conquest or political alliance, or a combination of both. The extension of Lo's brotherhood to Mao-ern, for example, had been a successful military campaigns supported by its alliance from within.[51] But, Salaman, Chu-ta-ya and other places seemed to have joined Lo's brotherhood by themselves.

The district head of Sinaman, Kapitan Bapah Wu had long been recognized as the absolute authority of Sinaman by the Panembahan of Mampawa before the birth of Lan-fang. He was invited to join Lo's

---

50. Schaannk, p.577.

These measures of austerity exercised by the Chinese *kongsi* in wartime may also be part of the Chinese military tradition. The *Wu-ei chi-yao* enumerates thirteen bans on normal activities in the town which was besieged. See Herbert Franke, 'Siege and Defense of Towns in Medieval China' in Kierman & Fairbank, eds., *Chinese Ways in Warfare*, New York, 1974, p.159.

51. Lo, p.138.

brotherhood and helped Lo to expand the territory of Lan-fang to the district of Mampawa.[52] Sinaman was made a province in the federation. The President resided in the capital, Mondor. But the office of the vice-President was in Sinaman. Mao-ern was made a prefecture administered by a major Kapitan or *Ma-yao Chia-pi-tan*. All the other districts in the federation each had a kapitan as its head administrator.[53]

The President of each administrative district in Lan-fang was assisted by a vice-President, a *Wu-ko* (junior elder brother) and a *Lao-ta* (the elder). These four men apart, there must be a treasurer or *ts'ai-ku* in each district administration. For example, in *Shan-hsin* gold mine, Chang Ah-chai who was originally the mine head before the birth of the Lan-fang *kongsi*, had now become the treasurer of Shan-hsin.[54] However, only the treasurer and kapitans were paid out of the *kongsi* fund, and *Lao-ta* and *Wui-ko* were honorary titles.[55] It seemed that each district administration evolved from a brotherhood in origin, such as the Lang-ho camp with five-man administration. There was a revolutionary change that characterized Lan-fang. After their admittance into the territory of Lan-fang, each of them ceased to be a single brotherhood by itself but only a district of Lan-fang. None of the old brotherhoods or *kongsi* retained its name. Neither the Lang-ho camp nor the Four Big families *kongsi* retained their names after the birth of Lan-fang, which was the extension of one brotherhood to the rest. In contrast, the Ho-shun was formed by an alliance of fourteen independent extended brotherhoods or *kongsi*, each retaining its own name and autonomy.

52. Lo, p.38.
53. Lo, p.158.
54. Lo, p.139.
55. Lo, p.141. De Groot, p.128.

Chapter 6

KONGSI EROSION AND THE KONGSI IN HISTORY

1. Discord Struck by the Growth of *Towkay* Influence

The birth of Ho-shun (Harmonious Agreement) and Lan-fang (Orchid Fragrance) was a watershed in the growth of Chinese political institutions overseas. While the American people were getting rid of monarchy and aristocracy and remodelling their political institutions, in this part of the world, West Borneo, the Hakka Chinese were also building a democratic life. All sources agree that administration of the *kongsi* at all levels was a representative government of a kind. It owed no inspiration to the West, nor to the rebellious tradition of Chinese peasantry.

The foundation of a Chinese *kongsi* had been its free institution that the *kongsi* officers must spend most of their time living in the *kongsi* house with the *kongsi*-mine miners. They had the same meals with the coolies on the mat. Every coolie considered himself a master of the house. During his Sinkawan visit, Earl's proposal to open a commercial intercourse with the British aroused a noisy discussion among the coolies:[1]

> The court-house was now filled with half-naked Chinese, each of whom considered himself authorized to join in the discussion which ensued, and endeavoured to make himself heard above his neighbour. The noise at least became perfectly deafening, and I was glad to escape it; under the plea of wishing to inspect the town.

In the discussion were not only the *kongsi*-mine coolies but also the *towkay* members in town. When a matter of significance unexpec-

---

1. Earl, p.208. Purcell, p.424.

tedly arose, all the *kongsi* members gather in the *kongsi*-house to hold a general meeting. Thus, the town was almost deserted by the men, "who were all in the court-house, and the shops were in the meantime taken care of by the women, many of whom were Chinese, though the majority of them were Dayaks."[2]

The *kongsi* officers lived with their wives in the *kongsi*-house. The *kongsi* coolies, however, for the most part were unmarried. The married ones lived in their own houses.[3] The pay of *kongsi* officers was generally higher than that of coolies. We have mentioned the salaries of district *kongsi* officers in the last chapter. The officers in the central government fetched even higher salaries. In the Ho-shun *kongsi*-house at Montrado, every *T'ing-chu*, the representative sent by each member *kongsi*, was paid 80 florins a month.[4]

With such a *kongsi*-house tradition, there was absolutely no ground for any individual, however outstanding, to claim a throne, especially when each member was his own master in the *kongsi*. However, the force of Lo's personality was said to have persuaded his admirers, including officers and coolies, to propose him a throne. Lo Fang-po, like Washington who in 1782 had twice rejected the proposal that he ought to be king,[5] declined the offer.[6] Washington's refusal understandably stemmed from his firm belief in democracy. What gave ground for Lo's rejection was his commitment to the brotherhood and its philosophy. He saw in the establishment of Lan-fang in foreign soil not his personal achievement but the success that crowned the collective efforts of his brotherhood. He, therefore, disdained the idea of proclaiming himself king which appeared unworthy and selfish to him.[7]

In fact, had he proclaimed the crown, he would undoubtedly have been dethroned by a revolt from the ranks sooner or later. Happily for

2.   Earl, p.210.
3.   Posewitz, T., p.361.
4.   Schaannk, p.570.
5.   John R. Alden, *Pioneer America*, London, 1966, p.98.
6.   Lo, p.38.
7.   Ibid.

himself and Lan-fang, he did not. However, in 1777 when Lan-fang possessed a vast territory and spheres of influence and a population of thirty to forty thousands, a new name had to be adopted to distinguish Lan-fang itself and its President. A consensus was achieved that the *kongsi* was distinguished by the name *Ta-tsung-chih* (presidential system, or perhaps 'Republic'), and to himself by the title *Ta-tsung-ch'ang* (the great president).[8]

It was also possible that only to outsiders, Lo used the title *Ta-wang* (which in general means king in Chinese, but in this particular context, governor), or the *Ta-wang* of Pontianak.[9] The title put Lo on par with the high position of the Dutch Governor, whose governorship was also through the election by the officers, as they thought. The term *Ta-wang* here, too, had a history. The Dutch governor was traditionally called *Ta-wang* by the overseas Chinese in Indonesia, this being so with both the *Annals* and the *Chinese Chronology on Batavia*.[10] By using the same title, the men of the *kongsi* must have seen Lan-fang as the equal of the Dutch Indies Company.

Another title that the president of the *kongsi* used to outsiders was *Panglima*. Between 1819 and 1822, during the conflict between the Dutch and the Chinese, the President or Kapitan-china of Mandor, Sung Cha-po was known to the Dutch as Panglima Tjap. Panglima in Malay means commander-in-chief. In 1822, when the *kongsi* negotiated peace with the Dutch, the Dutch insisted on a re-election of the whole of the leadership, and in particular, the resignation of the anti-Dutch Panglima, Tjap. It was accepted and thus a pro-Dutch leadership was formed by Kapitan-Demang Liu Tai-erh. Liu was sworn into office under the supervision of the Dutch Commissioner who handed over the great seal of the *kongsi* to him.[11]

This change of leadership was to have a far-reaching impact in Lan-fang. Peace was retained at a very high cost. Lan-fang sovereignty

---

8. Lo, p.39.
9. Lo, p.159.
10. *Kai-pa Li-tai Shih-chi* (The early accounts of the Chinese in Batavia), in JSSS, Vol.ix, pt. 1, p.27.
11. Veth, Vol.2, p.80

and independence was lost although its autonomy remained. Criticism of this expensive and fragile peace was aired in a folk saying: "What a blunder in Cha-po's administration that Tai-erh was entrusted with the power of district head! How ignorant and naive we all were that our flag pole was flying the Dutch flag!"[12] The apportion of blames seemed not limited to the leadership alone. The rank and file, whose consent on a matter of such importance must have been sought by the leadership, also take their share of responsibility.

The purity of the *kongsi* institution was, as noted by De Groot, eroded by this political change too. The political change enhanced the influence of the Kapitan over the electorate to a very large extent. The reason was that:[13]

> Under the changed circumstance, the dignitary was naturally the adviser in matter of the appointment of the kapitans, and he became the representative of the will of the Dutch government before the electorate. Indeed, in later years, his influence had grown so strong that the appointment of the lesser heads was entirely in his hands.

It was followed by a more serious erosion of the *kongsi* institution in later years. The residential tradition of officers was broken by the increasingly influential *towkay* groups whose interest were largely outside the *kongsi*. In Lan-fang, Yeh Teng-hui was the first to break it. During his presidency (1843-1845), he lived in his own shop instead of the *kongsi*-house. The *Annals* say that he only turned up to attend something important to the *kongsi*.[14] Criticisms of him by the *History* is even more blunt and direct: "He had completely neglected *kongsi* affairs."[15]

His successor, Liu Ting or Liu Chien-hsin who took office in 1846 made deeper and wider breaches in *kongsi* traditions. He renamed Lan-fang after a personal name of his – Chien-hsin.[16] Indications were that the erosion of the very foundation of *kongsi* – the *kongsi*-house tradi-

---

12. Lo, p. 153.
13. De Groot, pp. 128, 129.
14. Lo, p. 144.
15. Lo, p. 154.
16. Lo, p. 154.

tion – certainly caused a decline of Lan-fang. The *kongsi*-house fell into ruin due to neglect. The *kongsi* suffered a defeat from the Dayaks in Landak. The members were all demoralized, and there was a decline of population and income partly as a result of war destruction and partly because of the breaches of traditions.[17]

In Montrado, the increasing influence of *towkay* groups within the *kongsi* also wore away part of the free institutions of the *kongsi*. Some rich merchants who owned the small market-town *Shang-fu-tou*, were said to have rescued Ta-kang (the great port) *kongsi*, to which they belonged, from bankruptcy by pouring in their money. They were members of Wu, Huang and Cheng clans. Kuan Ming-po, a wine distiller, had also once saved Ta-kang from a financial crisis which paralysed its mine operation.[18] By pulling the *kongsi* through financial crises, the *towkay* groups gained more access to the leadership of Ta-kang.

They were given privileges that members of their clans should be placed in the *kongsi* mines' administrations. In a *kongsi* mine, one of the two mineheads or *huo-ch'ang*, one of the three treasurers or *ts'ai-k'u* must come from the surname groups of Huang, Wu or Cheng. Again out of the eight foremen or *ting-kung*, two were distributed to Wu, two to Huang, two to Cheng and only one left to any other surname groups. In a small mine there usually were four positions of foreman, of which Wu, Cheng and Huang clans each owned one respectively and left one to the minorities.[19]

The rise of *towkay* groups in the *kongsi* must have begun very early. During his visits to Montrado, Earl noted in April 1834 that:[20]

A company of individuals generally club together to work a mine, two or more of the shareholders being appointed directors, these latter generally being wealthy merchants, who purchase the shares of the miners at a risk, supplying them with food and opium. I could not

17. Lo, p.154.
18. Schaannk, p.571.
19. Schaannk, p.572.
20. Earl, p.286.

learn exactly the proportion in which the gold is distributed after being washed, but believe it to be nearly as follows:–

The government claims one-fourth, and of the remainder, the shares of the washer are two-thirds greater than those of the labourers who are only employed in mining.

This, of course, was a private partnership in the *kongsi* and not the *kongsi* mine itself. The leaders of private mines, usually wealthy merchants or *towkays*, wrested control from the miners by purchasing their shares. At first the rich *towkays* made loans to private miners at a high rate of interest, 24 to 36 per cent. When private miners were unable to pay out the debts, the *towkays* continued to lend money to them "but under harder conditions, demanding also some of the shares for themselves."[21] The rich *towkays* may have gained control over *kongsi* mines by making loans to them at high interest rates.

Kongsi mines did not have to pay tax to the *kongsi* government but only to contribute part of their profits to the *kongsi* fund. Private mines were taxed by the *kongsi* government. The tax had been varied from 1 florin to 6 florins per miner per month, depending on the yield of gold.[22] In Montrado, the number of private miners, according to Schaannk's estimate, was 1,200.[23] Doubtlessly, the total which included those in outlying colonies of Ta-kang must have been larger than this.

It is not clear when the new system of representation by surname groups began. Possibly, it occurred in 1848 during the presidency of Kuan Chih-I, a heavily built man with great intelligence. His success in using force to silence the vociferous party of miners of *kongsi* mines brought a period of relative peace to *Ta-kang*.[24] Since then the influence of *kongsi* mine workers was sagging. In 1850, Chen Hung-jen succeeded him. Only this succession and not those earlier ones was evidence of a sort that the new system was implemented.

Before the presidency of Kuan Chih-I, towkay groups in Ta-kang were unlikely to wield vast power. The rein of government remained

---

21. Posewitz, p.360.
22. Schaannk, p.599.
23. Ibid.
24. Schaannk, p.551.

held by the *kongsi*-mine miners. Their war efforts, more than anything else, contributed to what Ta-kang had become – the government of the whole of Montrado and a population of 30,000 to 50,000. By 1837, all the other member *kongsi* had been either merged into Ta-kang or driven out of Montrado. The powerful voice of the *kongsi*-mine workers dictated policy. Their mounting influence even resented the President. Wen Kuan-shou, who felt his presidential power unduly eclipsed by them, resigned in 1839.[25]

However, less than a decade later, their influence became thinned by the power of money. The men of money were the *towkay* groups, whose interest were not always in concert with that of *kongsi* miners. Although they and *kongsi*-mine workers alike were members of the extended brotherhood – the *kongsi*, they worked for their own account. Their ties with the *kongsi* were only the taxes and the authorities of the *kongsi* government on them. They did not live in the *kongsi*-house but their own in town, not paid by the *kongsi* but by the profits of their own business. Included among them were private owners of wine distilleries, opium dens, gambling booths, vegetable gardens, pigsties, shophouses and private mines. A few, like Kuan Ming-po, were very wealthy; but most of them were not.

Wealthy or not, the life of the *towkays* was the envy of mine coolies, who either worked for the *kongsi* or the *towkays*. Only one-tenth of miners had wives and their own houses.[26] *Towkays* in the town, on the other hand, were far better off. The rich ones are said to have kept concubines in different houses.[27] The life of the not so rich *towkays* was also blessed with the earthly bliss of their women, whose exotic beauty elicited admiration from both Earl and De Rees. The large-footed Dayak wives of the Chinese *towkays* appear under the pen of Earl:[28]

> The countenances of the Dayak women, if not exactly beautiful, are
> generally extremely interesting ... In form they are unexceptionable,

25. Schaannk, p.549.
26. Veth, Vol.1, p.314.
27. De Rees, p.53.
28. Earl, p.259.

and the Dayak wife of a Chinese whom I met with at Sinkawan, was, in point of personal attractions, superior to any eastern beauty who has yet come my observation ... Many of the Chinese on the west coast of Borneo are married to Dayak women, and their exemplary conduct both as wives and mothers, is very highly spoken of.

The mixed blood Chinese women borne by them, according to De Rees, excelled the pure Malay and Javanese in height and beauty.[29] Not infrequently the Chinese *towkays* took the parents or the whole families of their wives to live with them.[30] It was the Chinese custom that a gift of money to the family of the bride must be given by the man who asked for her hand. The money gift of betrothal varied from one to four taels of gold, or 80 to 320 florins.[31] Marriage was certainly expensive in West Borneo, where it was virtually only the elder Chinese *towkays* in town, mostly in their 50s and 60s, who wore wedding rings.[32]

Life without women had a bad influence on the morality of mine coolies, although it could, on the other hand, arouse their nostalgia and stimulate them to work doubly hard for their goals in life.[33] These Chinese coolies, intent on settling down after working in the mines for a long time to save up money, left the mines and the *kongsi*-house. They moved into town to open a shop or to practise a trade.[34] They became *towkays* themselves, and although not necessarily prospering at least lived in relative comfort and pleasure. The change to *towkays* was an upward move for the coolies, indeed to whom life in mines and the *kongsi*-house offered no comfort nor pleasure.

What was there was a brotherhood and hard work and austerity to share. Early in the morning at four o'clock the mine coolies got up to work until an interval of rest from 11 to 1, and then they proceeded on until sunset. Five meals a day were provided on the account of the *kongsi*. In the usual days, meals consisted of rice, salted and dried fish,

29. De Rees, p.49.
30. Earl, pp.293,294. Jackson, p.44.
31. De Rees, p.51.
32. Ibid.
33. Veth, Vol.1, p.314.
34. De Rees, p.51.

and a drink from the decoction of *gojaver* leaves. Tea and pork were served only on the day of gold-washing or pay-day, and on Chinese festivals which were celebrated with feasts and banquets.[35] Without sexual love, a large part of the coolies solaced themselves with the indulgence in wine, opium or gambling when they got their pay.

The conflicting interests of *towkay* groups and *kongsi* miners tore the *kongsi* further and further apart. The interest of *kongsi* coolies lay entirely in the *kongsi*-house. Through distinction in war, coolies were rewarded with shares in the *kongsi* mines. A new member or *Hsin'k'o* could also become shareholder after a year working in the *kongsi*-mine. The old coolies who had retired from work were given a share each for their long service to the *kongsi*.[36] The profits of *kongsi*-mines after setting part of it for the *kongsi* fund, were divided by the shareholders or mine workers. When the profit was huge, everyone of them could expect a bonus to be added to their dividend.[37] The *kongsi*-house provided them a roof under the sky, meals, democratic life and brotherhood and a share in gain and loss.

Towkays, unless they had bought a share in the *kongsi* mine, were entirely on their own. The *kongsi*-house, furthermore, levied on them a capitation tax and a household tax to the amount of 2 florins a year, from which the coolies, however, were exempted. In addition, all the *towkays* had to pay a tax for their private business, from which the coolies, of course, were free. A private miner had to pay 1 to 6 florins in tax a year to the government or *kongsi*-house, a private farmer 2 florins. The private business taxes for the *towkay* of wine distillery, pawn-shop, gambling-house, and artisan, ranged from 1 to 32 florins.[38] The *kongsi*-house raising taxes on them for revenue often injured the growth of their money trees. Indirect taxes on them were high too; 1 florin for each pig slaughtered, for each gantang (= 3.125 kg) of oil 5 duits (1 duit = $\frac{1}{60}$ florin), each gantang of rice 2 duits.[39] The *towkays*

35. Veth, Vol.1, p.339.
36. Schaannk, p.572.
37. Schaannk, p.573.
38. Schaannk, pp.599,600.
39. Veth, Vol.1, pp.321,322.

grumbled at high taxation more especially when war and overspending by the *kongsi*-house imposed extra taxes on them.

The *towkay* domination of the *kongsi*-house ended the political partnership of *towkays* and coolies. The rise of *towkay* influence undermined the free institution that the *kongsi* government and laws once stood for. Clanism and racialism creeped into the law of the *kongsi* widening the gap between the *towkays* and coolies. The new order favoured the large surname groups and China-born Chinese. Members of such clans supplied a new gentry in the region. The new law and justice were made in their favour. For example, the penalty for the murder of any member of the *towkay* elite was certainly death sentence, but only a fine of 720 florins and caning for killing a member of small clans. When the victim was a half-caste Chinese or Pan-Tang-fan, his life was scarcely worth half a package of red tobacco and 48 florins in the new law.[40]

When clanism raised its ugly head in the new order, the half-caste Chinese organized underground opposition. In a number of places in Ta-kang they formed their own secret brotherhood.[41] It was only a matter of time before they would rise in revolt. The 1850s saw more discords among the already divided Chinese community in Montrado. Ta-kang was confronted with the Dutch invasion. The *kongsi*-house sent a delegation to the Dutch offering unconditional surrender and control over the *kongsi's* domestic affairs. The *towkay* elite wanted peace at any price whereas San Tien-hui (three dots brotherhood) of the underprivileged advocated armed resistance. The *towkay* elite won their way. Ta-kang surrendered.[42] The lack of will in the *kongsi*-house to offer resistance brought an end to Chinese autonomy that had lasted almost a century in West Borneo.

In Mandor, Chinese autonomy and public accessibility, though much diluted by the growing Dutch influence, lingered on for another two decades until 1875. The public accessibility of the *kongsi* government continued to survive the erosion from the top and from outside

40. Schaannk, p.582.
41. Schaannk, p.587.
42. Irwin, *Nineteenth Century Borneo*, (Leiden, 1955), pp.168,169.

over time. The democratic spirit that remained in Lan-fang was still very much alive:[43]

> Every head, including the president, *Kapitan*, was accessible to the public on every day and in any hour; not a shadow of submission was shown by any farmer or coolie when meeting on the road, but only politeness in their affable and intimate conversation. No head-man would feel displeased when walking on the road nearby his residence any resident farmer came to talk with him. In short, the people always held, whether they let it show or not, the heads with a harmonious mixture of respect and free intimacy.

As my study deals only with the origins of Chinese *kongsi*, I should leave the story there. The intense growth of *kongsi* mining in Sarawak, Malay states and South Thailand well into the late nineteenth century, and the far-reaching impact of *kongsi* government after this, are, however, a story that should be told elsewhere.

2. *Kongsi*: Its Place in History

One can hardly exaggerate the significance of the emergence of *kongsi* federations in West Borneo, which was to shape Chinese life in Southeast Asia for one and a half centuries. But as a political structure, what is it? Is it as a wide range of scholars such as Veth, De Groot, Schlege and Lo Hsiang-lin see it, some form of federal republic? Or, is it merely the large political groups in the mining districts, as those who reject the first view would prefer to have it? To answer this one must know what is democracy, and further more, what form of democracy the *kongsi* is and what form it is not? I think a controversy of this kind is futile. However, while avoiding the comparison of the *kongsi* with modern republicanism and 'democracy', I should also point out that the second view which leaves *kongsi* federations in a limbo of vague-ness and ambiguity, is no solution either.

Therefore, I suggest a third approach, which rejects western ter-minology for this completely Chinese model of political state. In other words, we should not try to fit the *kongsi* government to western ter-

---

43. De Groot, p.140

minology, nor to western models of history – the chief points of origins for western terminology. And indeed, it is all too often misleading to translate histories very different from that of the West into western terminology. More especially, historians who uncritically apply western models of history to other parts of the world, would in so doing, remind one of a Chinese proverb which says: "Cutting the feet in order to fit the shoes".

Nor do I advocate an uncritical acceptance of the autonomy of Asian history, especially not to the exclusion of some convergence of both Asian and European histories, such as trade and cultural contacts which go far back in time. But *kongsi* government, such as it was, was built by the Chinese who were uninfluenced by western ideas and experience. Nevertheless, whether *kongsi* government is uniquely Chinese in West Borneo, or might be found in other parts of the world in history, is a question which I prefer to leave open.

Most early writers on this subject were impressed by the democratic rights of the members in a *kongsi*. Not surprisingly, they freely compared *kongsi* with republics. Temminck, for example, wrote in 1847: "These market towns *kongsi* of Borneo Chinese which are known as *kongsis*, vary in size of population; ... These little republics formed in the common interest of adventurers obliged to defend themselves against the Dayak hordes, and the Mohamedan princes".[44] *Kongsi* government, likewise, struck Veth as something of a republic which arose, undoubtedly, from the hope of the Chinese to gain strength by this vehicle in their resistance against Malay extortion and the Dayaks who initially felt hostile towards these foreigners, who came by repeated influxes into their midst.[45]

De Groot holds a similar view. Furthermore, he tries to interpret the term *kongsi* as a synonym for republicanism in Chinese:

Already the term *kongsi* itself, or, according to the Hakka dialect, *koeng-sji* or *kwoeng-sze*, indicates perfect republicanism. It means

---

44. Temminck, *Coup-doel General sur les Possession Neerlandais sur l'Inde Archipelagique*, Tome 2, (Leide, 1847), pp.167-174.
45. Veth, Vol.2, pp.305,306.

exactly administration (*Si*) of something which is of collective or common interest (*kong*). It has, therefore, also been used by large corporations and commercial firms. But when used as the term for the political organizations in West Borneo, it should be interpreted as meaning an organization for governing the republic or the *res pulica*.[46]

Elsewhere, in the *Beknopte Encyclopaedië Van Nederlandsche Oost-Indië*, the term is clearly defined as government by a general public or administration of affairs that belong to the common interests.[47] Of course, That is not all. Both the encyclopaedia and Veth have pointed out that *kongsi* is, at the same time, a title used by administrators who were elected by ordinary members in the *kongsi*.[48]

As has been shown in the first section of the third chapter, the usage of the term *kongsi* has been found in the ships of the Cheng regime, as early as 1683. The term it seems, referred to ship officers who shared cargoes among themselves, as distinct from the *Mu-shao*, the sailors who again shared theirs. But when this term migrated to Bangka and West Borneo, the usage changed hands from ship officers to mining officers. The emergence of *kongsi* government in the 1770s, however, gave the term a new meaning, a radical change in continuity.

This new form of overseas Chinese government did not part with all Chinese traditions. In fact, as has been demonstrated in previous chapters, the roots of *kongsi* government lay in the traditions of Chinese partnership systems and brotherhood societies, and in particular, that of a combination of both. While the Cheng regime can be seen as an extension of a single partnership, it was not an extended brotherhood. It was, nevertheless, an old political framework which more or less still retained a legacy of the Chinese imperial system. But, in sharp contrast, *kongsi* government has departed sharply from this orthodoxy of Chinese political traditions. It has extended the equality of partnership and brotherhood to all members. It was, in this respect, a

46.   De Groot, p.138.
47.   Beknopte Encyclopaedië Van Nederlandsche-Indië, (Leiden, 1921) p.254.
48.   Veth, Vol.1, p.319.

revolutionary change in the Chinese political philosophy, which unfortunately did not have a Thomas Paine to articulate it.

The revolutionary significance of *kongsi* government was not fully appreciated, as it was interpreted as the *k'o-chang* system, in China, until one century and a half later. Only then there was a new appreciation of *kongsi* government among the generation who had been won over by western ideas of democracy and republicanism. But the appreciation of this generation was only partial. In 1911, in the first year of the Chinese Republic, Lin Feng-chao hailed the advent of the *Lan-fang Ta-tsung-chi* (the Presidential System of the Lan-fang *kongsi*) as the earliest example of Chinese republicanism. He says: "The Lan-fang *kongsi* was indeed a democratic republic, but, because a hundred years ago the Chinese people did not know the precedence of America and France, it was seldom talked about as such a thing of great importance."[49] More specifically is his comment on the time-scale used by the Lan-fang *kongsi*:

> In the chronological year of Huang-Ti 4471 and that of Chien-lung 42, Lo Fang-po from Kuantung Mei-hsien had occupied Pontianak of Borneo. He was elected by the public as the *Ta-Dang Tsung-chang* (the President of Great China). In this year, he founded thus the first year of Lan-fang. The use of Huang-Ti's chronological year was to praise the people of the Lan-fang country. Why praise them? It was because they were able to follow the example of Huang-Ti to defeat barbarians. Again, by using the term *Kung-chi* (public election) here, the author meant to demonstrate the republican nature of the Lan-fang *kongsi*. Similarly, by using the term *chien-yüan* (founding the first chronological year for a new dynasty), it indicated independence from the Manchou government. The history of the revolution of the overseas Chinese began with Fang-po.[50]

In the glow of his radical nationalism, Lin could see nothing but the resemblance to the republic in the *kongsi*. Twenty years later, Lo Hsian-ling became interested in mining the history of the *kongsi*. In 1948, Lü Chen-yü became aware of the significance of the *kongsi* in

49. Lo, p.158.
50. Lo, p.149.

Chinese history from a Marxist point of view. Lo, who belongs to tradi-tional scholarship,[51] seems content with a parallel with the western republic in the Chinese *kongsi*. He does not ask himself where this form of Chinese 'republic' derived its originality. Lü, at the other end of the Chinese intellectual spectrum, is a distinguished Marxist his-torian in the generation of modern scholarship. Nevertheless, his con-ceptual tool – the Marxist system of history – remains one of Western terminology. He sees in the *kongsi* an embodiment of the ideas of the Chinese *shi-min* or Chinese equivalent of European burgher class.[52] The appreciation of the *kongsi* as it actually existed in modern Chinese scholarship has been equally Eurocentric, although it stemmed from the Chinese themselves.

All the same, both Western and Chinese scholarship failed to ap-preciate that the revolutionary significance of *kongsi* government lies entirely in being something without parallel with the West. In some sense, *kongsi* government was a part of Chinese popular traditions – partnership and brotherhood. But in West Borneo, it stood out quite clearly as a Chinese modern form of representative government, an unique contribution of the Chinese to the art of government in the world.

Modern western scholarship, however, does not fail to see the democratic characters of *kongsi* government. Recent researchers such as Jackson and Barbara Ward have both placed great emphasis on the essential feature of the *kongsi* – authority delegated upwards from be-low.[53] This is true. But it is not this that makes the *kongsi* revolutionary.

More significant than this are five essential features that contribute much of what a *kongsi* government has been. First of all, it is the short tenure of office for the administrators – theoretically at least, four months. Once their office expired, they had to return to work like anybody else in the mine.[54] There was no soil in the minefield for the

51. Wang Gungwu, *The Origins of Civilization: An Essay on Chinese Scholarship in Transition*, p.17.
52. Lü Chien-yü, *Chien-ming Chung-kuo Tung-shih* (A Concise History of China), (Peking, 1956) p.682.
53. Jackson, p.66.

growth of bureaucratization, which has become a modern disease infecting almost the whole world.

Secondly, administrators were all dismissible by ordinary members during their term of office. This shows the extent to which *kongsi* members could exercise checking power over the executives of government. Not only was a voice in the *kongsi*-house enjoyed by every member of the *kongsi*; if necessary the electorate could remove the office holders from power at any time they pleased. There can be no doubt that:[55]

> When they (officers), however, gave cause for the discontent of their constituents, they would surely be dismissed even during their office, and they were obliged to drop their office when it happened.

Kongsi government is most remarkable for the consensus process that effectively limited bureaucratic power. It was a vital aspect of *kongsi* government that the administration was controlled by the public dictation of policy through the consensus process.[56] Consensus or popular consent formed the core of *kongsi* philosophy and government – harmonious agreement. One step outside the consensus, the administration was exceeding its powers. Should there arise anything important beyond what had been agreed upon by the consensus, a new consensus to deal with it must be sought by *kongsi*-house. Here, there was only executive power in the hands of the *kongsi*-house. The public, constitutionally though not in writing, had the last words on legislation and policy formulation. This was the vestige of its partnership origins that the headmen had nothing but executive power.

Kongsi government also offers a fine example of what we nowadays call collective leadership. In its truest sense, it was far more collective than its anachronistic equivalents. Decision on important matters must be collective, must be from *kongsi*-house and not the Kapitan alone, no matter how capable and influential he was. For example, Kapitan Lo-phai, whose dynamic leadership earned him the

---

54. Veth, Vol.1, p.319.
55. Ibid.
56. Veth, Vol.1, p.320.

confidence of the people and ten years of office, was even more faithful to the principle of collective leadership.[57] Not just because of the force of tradition did he refuse to determine the British proposal for a trade relationship in April 1843, but also because he himself did not wish so. This proposal was therefore put before a council meeting for a collective decision.

The collective leadership that consisted in *kongsi* government made a profound impression on Earl:[58]

> That which they have adopted appears to be well suited to their situation, the territory being divided into districts, each of which is governed by several representatives, elected by the people, every male inhabitant having a vote. The representatives, or Kung Se, elect the governor, who has the direction of all the affairs of the territory, domestic and foreign, but he is expected to consult the Kung Se when transacting any business of importance. The latter are entrusted with the administration of justice in their respective districts, but capital offences are always referred to the governor. They continued in office as long as it suits the pleasure of their constituents, who on suspicion of misconduct, will depose the obnoxious members and elect others in their room.

Later in 1847, Temminck also noted this:[59]

> The executive power of the *kongsi* community has devolved to a Chinese carrying the title of captain. In all extraordinary matters, this man is bound to call an assembly of the clerks who must acquaint the members of their societies with the affairs in question; the opinion adopted by the members must be communicated to the captain who then acts on it.

In other words, the President had only executive power, with regard to both policy and justice, and so with the whole of the administration. *Kongsi* officers were seen by the rank and file as people

---

57. Earl, p.291.
   During ten years of his presidency, he and his family lived in the *Kongsi*-house, which, according to Schaannk, was an exception among the presidents before him. Schaannk, p.545.
58. Earl, pp.290,291.
59. Temminck, p.397.

who carried out what they have all agreed and not a ruling elite to tell them what they should or should not do. Every one of them, as an equal partner and brother in the *kongsi*, saw himself as his own master, and enjoyed a voice in *kongsi* politics. It was they who were the masters of the *kongsi*-house and not the administrators. Their loyalty to the *kongsi* sprang from a belief of collective self-mastery, which in no way diminished in strength the bold vision of extended brotherhood.[60]

A belief in universal brotherhood was old in Chinese life. A very old Chinese saying, probably as old as ancient Greek stoicism, was that within all the corners of the earth every man is a brother. What was new was not the philosophy itself but the practices of extended brotherhood and collective self-direction. And what was the most exciting breakthrough in *kongsi* government was that it was not only a government by representation but also a government by public opinion, or popular consent. Neither did the public see their representatives as the masters of the *kongsi*-house, nor *kongsi* officers themselves did so. They always sought for collective ideas and public opinion in the process of government. Veth writes of this unique contribution of Chinese *kongsi* in West Borneo to the art of government in history, which, however, is not widely known even now:[61]

> In special cases, in which general regulations or guidelines are not provided, the central government called on the clerks of the districts for consultation. If they still could not settle it, they subjected the problem to the opinions of their constituents. The opinions were then reported to the *kongsi*-house which accordingly adjusted their measures. In case the central government abused its power, it ran a great risk of being overthrown by a popular commotion, in which the ranks took their rights into their hands. On such occasions, which fortunately did not happen frequently, general meetings were held and most of them were so turbulent and chaotic that they ended with bloodshed.

---

60. In Chinese dissent traditions, whether of popular or intellectual, the absence of the notion of negative freedom is apparent. On the other hand, the fruits of European civilizations seem to be civil rights established on the notion of negative freedom. See Isaiah Berlin, *Four Essays on Liberty*, (London, 1969) pp.131-136.
61. Veth, Vol.1, p.320.

Kongsi government as it was, is indeed a political philosophy, or a collective way of thinking in action, rather than in abstraction. It is a system of political ideas, which was evolved from the practices of brotherhood and partnerships by the overseas Chinese, and not from the Utopian scheme of any great philosopher. The founders constructed this form of government upon their notion of social justice (*kung-ping*), for the Chinese until then were alien to the concept of democracy, but subsumed it within social justice. Their notion of social justice was a philosophy of public spirit, which was as old as the origin of Chinese civilization itself. An old Chinese saying, for instance, that it is to the public that the whole of China belongs, (*T'ien-hsia Wei-kung*) has long been the inspiration of the Chinese dissent tradition. Criticism by outspoken reformist officials and scholars alike against the tyranny of the emperor and the monarchy system itself mainly stemmed from this tradition.

But of course thus far the philosophy had not been translated into a political system that shaped the life of the Chinese people, who saw only dynasties rise and fall. It is only in West Borneo that the Chinese philosophy of public spirit was used as a conceptual tool in the construction of a new form of government, a government of collective self-direction. But then this political philosophy in action is not the Chinese philosophy of public spirit in general, but one that is particular. Particular, because it directly derived its inspiration from the Chinese popular traditions rather than Chinese intellectual traditions, whether of ancient sages or of contemporary reformist thinkers. Particular, also because its origins were with a happy marriage of brotherhood and partnership in Chinese life which formed the powerful idea of collective self-mastery.

By the time West Borneo evolved a *kongsi* system of government, the word *kongsi* was redefined by this maturing of the political philosophy behind the system. *Kongsi* became taken to mean a government of public spirit, public spirit in every sense of the word. In practice, the administration was the instrument of the consensus process. The power of directing the *kongsi*-house was wielded by the hands of the public through their direct participation, election, criticism and control of the administration, which had only executive power. This alone is significant. To world history the West supplied *democracy* from its traditions of civil rights. The overseas Chinese, alien to civil rights, contributed *kongsi* from their natural heritage of partnership and brotherhood. The *kongsi* is neither democracy nor republicanism. History should give the *kongsi* a place which is rightfully its own.

EPILOGUE

It has been nearly a decade and a half since I was engaged in the mining of the gold from the history of Chinese *kongsi* builders both in China itself and overseas through various Chinese, English, Japanese, and Dutch sources accessible. Historiographical however, the work has fortunately withstood the test of time and the flux of changes. It has remained a piece of pioneering work in English and hopefully this will blaze a trail for a historiography of "the Chinese century of Southeast Asia from 1740 to 1840" which witnessed a remarkable growth of Chinese influence in the smaller Asian states.[1] This was a period of independent *Kongsi* migration which continued throughout the eighteenth and into the nineteenth century, expanding with the Chinese junk trade. The junk trade flourished throughout Southeast Asia, as pointed out by Carl A. Trocki, enhanced by the traffic in goods produced by the Chinese *Kongsi* settlements scattered throughout the region, particularly tin, gold, pepper, and gambier.[2]

Perhaps more important is the question whether such a valuable history or tradition is already dead or still living with the Chinese, particularly those of overseas? In other word, is it no more than a fossil from the Chinese past no longer shaping the course of the Chinese political and economic developments both in Mainland China and Southeast Asia? Undoubtedly, the equality as represented by a

---

1. Antony Reid: "Historiogaphy Reflection on the Period 1750-1870 in Southeast Asia and Korea". Paper presented to the panel 'The Last Stand of Autonomous States in Southeast Asia and Korea' 1750-1870 at the 34th International Congress of Asian and North African Studies (ICANAS), Hong Kong, 22-28 August 1993, p. 8, 9.
2. Carl. A. Trocki: *Opium and Empire, Chinese Society in Colonial Singapore 1800-1910,* (Itaca, 1990), p. 32, 33.

combination of brotherhood and partnership during the "Chinese century" had long diminished if not completely disappeared in Southeast Asia. Since then there has not been any modern parallel in China that seems really close enough to have resembled the specie of the Chinese civil society that *Kongsi* once was until became extinguished by the emergence of that of towkay dominant *Kongsi*.

Nevertheless, *Kongsi* as a form of Chinese traditional partnership is, to my surprise, very much alive and well in Mainland China and a large part of Southeast Asia. While not without some sort of variations and adaptations as required by the change of times and circumstances, the very substance and essential features of the Chinese traditional partnership system are clothed under modern appearances and called by some different names hardly recognizable. But they are there all right, and still a formidable economic dynamism in the region.

The economic reforms introduced in China since 1979 have prevented it from falling the same fate as Soviet Russia and the Eastern Europe. But the uniqueness and the remarkable achievements of China's economic reform have been the result of its willingness to accommodate itself to reality, its readiness to draw inspirations and strength from the aged-old economic tradition called *Cheng-bao* system or a system to give extra profits to oneself by farming out the state targeted tax revenue. Thus a great variety of *Cheng-bao* systems was produced in the process of reviving with a vengeance old traditions in the name of economic reforms.[3] One of these variants of *Cheng-bao* systems emerged from the presently world renowned Shoudou Steel has become especially successful. The system is called *Chuan Yuan Cheng-bao* which involves every staff by giving them each a stake in the gain and loss of the whole enterprise. Whereas prior to 1990, the manager responsibility system where only the managers themselves are farming the state targeted revenues was far more universal and widespread throughout China. Most of them failed

---

3.　Fan Li 范蠡 : "Wei Shen Mo Chongkuo Neng, Tulian Pu Neng" 爲甚麼中國 能獨聯不能 (Why is it that China suceeds in economic reforms and yet the Ex-Soviet fails?) in 'Asia Pacific Rim page', *Sing Tao Daily* (5 November, 1992, Hong Kong).

dismally. But Shoudou Steel has been growing from strength to strength, thanks to the system which makes the whole enterprise virtually an extended, collective partnership. The system glues everyone to the enterprise by giving each an identity of interest between them and the enterprise. It is this identity of interest in the partnership which keeps alive the enthusiasm of the whole staff to offer ·numerous solutions and innovations to improve economic efficiency and to overcome problems of cost absorption. The partnership and the sense of being one's own master is the reason why the contract responsibility system's boosting effects on economic efficiency did not wear out as it did in the case of many other large and medium state enterprises.[4]

Chinese *Kongsi* as we know has been making its comeback in the form of an extended partnership in Shoudou since 1979. This extended partnership has now grown to 270,000 members of staff, an enormous multinational company of 149 subsidiaries, 57 joint ventures, and 34 foreign joint ventures. It has its own bank, a university, a fleet of ocean vessels, a research institute, construction teams, light industry, chemical industry, ship-building factory, hotels, garment factories with branches or joint ventures overseas.[5] Such a large scale of an extended partnership is, of course, beyond comparison. Even during the heyday of Chinese *kongsi* in West Borneo, none of them could boast as big though, regardless of their greater degree of civic participation of *kongsi* affairs.

---

4. Wang Tai Peng: "Shoudou Steel: The Top Chinese State Enterprise", unpublished paper, p. 14-18, December, 1991.
    Fan Li: 范蠡 "Shougan *Chuan-yuan Cheng-bao* Chi Wei Ho Cheng Kong?"首鋼全員承包制爲何成功 ? (Why the whole staff responsibility system of Shoudou Steel meets with success?) in 'Asia pacific Rim Page', *Sing Tao Daily*, (Hong Kong, 13 November, 1992)
5. Lin Fang 林芳 : "Shougan Chian Kong Siang Kang" 首鋼搶攻香港 (Shoudou Steel is establishing itself in Hong Kong) *China Times Weekly*, p. 9, (Hong Kong, 19 September, 1993).

Lately in China however, there has been a tremendous growth of *Long Min Gu Fen He Zhuo Zhi* (peasant co-operative share system).[6] This is clearly much more closely resembling the traditional Chinese partnership system of *kongsi* than the *Chuan Yuan Cheng Bao* system practised by Shoudou. While Shoudou partnership is only limited to the sharing of profits but not of ownership, the emerging "new" partnership system throughout the country is based on a collective ownership through pooling resources together by all the members of a village, instead of being based on state ownership. The Chinese Government is now pinning much of its hope on this spontaneous upsurge of the countryside reform to give the much needed impetus to its flagging agricultural economy and its diminished dynamism for changes.

Elsewhere in Southeast Asia however, the traditional Chinese partnership system has evolved into commercial empires of modern times as well. The so-called Liem investors for Indonesia has burst into the international scene as one of the most dynamic Southeast Asian conglomerate of diverse interests all over the world. In Indonesia, the holdings of the partnership include Bogasari Flour Mills, Indocement Tunggal Prakarsa and Cold Rolling Mill Indonesia. Overseas, the partnership is the biggest shareholder in Hongkong-based First Pacific.[7] At home the partnership is called Waringin Kancana group. Its total investment last year is estimated at US2.3 billion with a total turnover of US4.8 billion. The Liem partnership is also reported to have controlled 12 listed companies with a capitalization reaching US5 billion. 40% of its profits is derived from oversea sources.[8] Yet, unlike western MNCs or the great majority of Asian family controlled MNCs, the whole commercial empire has been owned by everyone but not any one in the partnership. It is a collective ownership.

---

6. For a detailed survey of the emerging Chinese peasant share co-operatives, see Huang Liang Tian, 黃良天 : "Zhoung Guo Nong Min Xiang Gao Chu Zhou – Nong Min Yu Gu Feng He Zuo Zhi" 中國農民，向高處走 — 農民與 股份合作制 in *Xing Guang Monthly* (Beijing, September 1993)
7. Adam Schwarz: "Empire of the Son", *Far Eastern Economic Review*, p. 47, 14 March, 1991.
8. See, *Chih Pen-chia* 資本家 (Forbes) (Hongkong, June 1993), p. 83.

The Liem partnership was founded in 1965 when Suharto just came into power. Soedono Salim, Djuhar Sutanto, and the sworn brother of President Suharto, Sudwikatamoto and Ibrahim Risjad, together formed a partnership known as the Liem investors in which Liem Sioe Liong had 40% stake, Djuhar another 40%, the rest 10% each. Sudwikatawono has been the direct link to President Suharto, and Ibrahim to the military. Both of them have served a useful purpose.[9] Djuhar who is given credit for building up the group's cement business in the 1970s came from the county of Hokchian same as Liem. Djuhar calls Liem *uncle* as Liem has been a close friend of Djuhar's late father.[10] Liem who left China at the age of 19 is certainly a traditional Chinese. Traditional Chinese commercial practices live with him. Little wonder that he has built his commercial empire upon the basis of the tradition Chinese partnership system. Prominent examples are partnerships with Mochtar Riady in banking, Cipta Wijaya in palm oil and milk products, Henry Probadi in chemicals and Robert Kuok in hotels and commodity trading. In all these partnerships, Liem has often taken a passive interest in business and let the other partners run the businesses. Such as it is, it is in fact a tradition of Shin-tu merchants who prospered on similar way of capital supply wedding with profit sharing and non-interference during the Ming dynasty period.

In much the same fashion, Robert Kuok too has built a no less enormous commercial empire world-wide than that of the Liem partnership. Starting from a partnership formed by all the family members of his brothers and cousins, he has enlarged it by including powerful political connections and wealthy and successful business partners such as Liem Sioe Liong, the late Ho Yao Kung of Singapore, Run Run Shaw of Hong Kong, the Chin family of the Bangkok Bank. It is only natural for him to do business through partnerships and never to go it alone. To him, an enterprise to be monopolized by a single

---

9.   Adam Schwarz, op. cit, p. 47.
10.   *Fu Pu Zian Ciao Feng Wu Chih*   福莆仙鄉僑風物誌   . (Biographies of the fellow countrymen of the Fuchou and Putien counties) (Singapore, 1992), p. 2.

person is absolutely unthinkable. More often than not he only holds 20% to 30% of the shares, and in some instances, as little as only 4% ownership of the enterprise or the group controlled by he himself.[11]

---

11. Zhou Shao Long 周少龍 Guo He Nien Zhuan 郭鶴年傳 (The Biography of Robert Kuok) (Hong Kong, 1993) p. 191, 193.

NOTE ON THE SOURCES

Yeh's *Annals* was first published by De Groot in 1895. The *Annals* covers in a brief manner the history of Lan-fang from 1777 to 1856. It was probably written in the 1860s or 1870s. Throughout this work, there is an obvious bias against the rival of Lan-fang–Ta-kang. Yeh also seems totally pro-Dutch and pro-Manchu in this writing.

Apart from the *Annals*, Lin's *History* is the only surviving Chinese historical document on Lan-fang, but it came out much later, in 1911. The value of this work is mainly the inclusion of the writing of Lo Fang-po himself. Again it is a republican interpretation of the *kongsi*, which I have pointed out in this book.

I have drawn heavily on De Groot, Schaannk, and Veth, in reconstructing the democratic life of the *kongsi*. All of them had personally visited West Borneo. While De Groot presented the Chinese point of view of Mondore, Schaannk projected that of Montrado. In collecting materials from the Chinese and Dayaks there, Schaannk had checked them with Veth who largely relied on Dutch official documents. But on the other hand, he also checked the mistakes of Veth in the light of his own findings, such as the coin of ho-shun 14 *kongsi*.

It is for this reason that I take exception to Irwin who classified them purely as secondary sources.

GLOSSARY

Ch'ang-chu 廠主	The official appointed by the Ch'ing Government to be in charge of the jurisdiction and taxation of a Yünnan copper mining settlement.
Ch'ang 廠	A remote mining settlement in Yünnan copper mines.
Ch'ang-Min 廠民	Miners in Yünnan copper mines.
Ch'u-hai 出海	Literally it means going out to the sea, refers to agent captains who owned no sea vessel but instead worked for a shipowner.
Ch'uan-chu 船主	Also *P'o-chu*, used to refer to a shipowner captain.
Chieh-lian 結連	Of a member of the West Borneo gold mining *kongsi*, literally it means linking up.
Chun-ssu 軍師	The elected military advisers of a *kongsi* which went to war.
Chai-chu 寨主	Field-forts commanders of warring *kongsi*.
Fen-ku ho-huo 分股會夥	A Chinese partnership system.
Fu-kan-shou 副綱首	Vice captain of a Chinese sea vessel.
Fu-tou-jen 副頭人	*Kongsi* leaders both of central level and district level.
Hsiao-huo-chi 小夥計	Of calling in Yünnan copper mines; meaning small partners.
Hsi-t'ou 錫頭	The leader of metal workers.
Hui 會	A form of miner brotherhood.
Hui-ti 會地	Literally the foundation of a brotherhood, usually refers to the admission fee for *kongsi* membership.

Hu-hsi 會心	Literally the heart of a brotherhood, refers to *kongsi* membership fee.
Hun 分	Referring to shareholders in a small mining partnership.
Huo-chang 伙長	Also *k'o-chang*, the leader of the crew in a Chinese sea vessel where the ship-merchants called their own leaders as such.
Huo-fang 伙房	A Yünnan mining settlement made of twenty to thirty people who built tents as their shelters. A headman of such mining settlement there and then.
I-fu 義夫	Miners in Yünnan copper mining.
Kapitan 甲必丹	Also *Chai-pi-tan*, the head of the Chinese community in a colonial city of Southeast Asia, usually appointed by the government.
Kai-hsiang kongsi	A pioneering *kongsi*.
K'o-t'ou 客頭	Also *k'o-chang*, the administrators elected of a *kongsi* usually with one- or two-year term of office. The elected head of a Chinese ship-merchant partnership.
K'o-shang 客商	Also *chuan-shang* 船商 , Ship merchants.
Kongsi 公司	Also *kung-ssu*, a Chinese partnership, in Bangka tin mining it was a title referring to the representatives of the court of Palembang.
K'uai-shang 儈商	Agent merchants working for some kind of specialized commercial guilds known as *ya-hang.* 牙行
Kuan-ku 管庫	The treasurer.
Kuan-shih 管事	The leader who supplied capital and recruited workers in Yünnan copper mining.
Kng-chi 公舉	Public election.
Kung-ping 公平	Social justice.
Lao-k'o 老客	Old member of Chinese mines.
Mi-fen 米分	A partnership to share profit according to the contribution of the shares in the form of rice.
Mu-shao 木梢	Refers to sailors in a trading junk of the Cheng kingdom.

Nam	Large Chinese gold mines in Sambas and Mampawa.
Nin-pan 領班	Overseers.
Pan-Tang-Fan 半唐蕃	Half-caste Chinese.
Po 伯	Almost invariably all presidents of Chinese mining brotherhoods in West Borneo carried the title Po, which was recognized by Malays as equivalent to Kapitan.
Shan-Sha 山砂	Chinese gold mining small partnership.
Shao-liao 砂寮	Huts which sheltered the Chinese gold miners in West Borneo.
Shih-mins 市民	Chinese equivalent of European burgher class.
Shih-fen 石分	A Chinese mining partnership identifical to *mi-fen*.
Ta-kang	(Great Port) one of the largest Chinese gold mining *kongsi* in West Borneo.
Ta-po-kung 大伯公	The great founder of a Chinese settlement or brotherhood.
Ta Wang 大王	The Dutch Governor was traditionally called *Ta Wang* by the overseas Chinese in Indonesia. The title was thus used by the Chinese in West Borneo to mean something of a Governor.
Ta-Dang Tsung-chang 大唐總長	Literally the President of Great China.
Ta-ko 大哥	The elder brother but usually referrring to the senior member in a brotherhood.
Ti-hsiung 弟兄	Brothers.
T'ien-ti Hui 天地會	Heaven and Earth Brotherhood.
T'ing 廳	A *kongsi*-house which was used as a stockade, a *Ta-po-kung* temple, a store-house and sleeping quarter by Chinese miners.
Ting-kung 鼎工	Foreman.
Tung-t'ou 銅頭	Mine-heads in Yünnan copper mines.
Tung-fu 銅戶	The people of the Yünnan copper mines.
Wei-ko Lao-ta 尾哥老大	Assistant headmen in a Chinese kongsi.
Yüeh-huo 月活	Monthly salaried workers.

SELECT BIBLIOGRAPHY

The selection here only includes sources cited in the book and work of particular interest to my discussion.

ASIAN LANGUAGE SOURCES

Chang Hsieh 張燮 . *Tung-hsi yang-k'ao* 東西洋考 (An Investigation of the Eastern and Western Oceans). 12 *chüan*. Originally published in 1618.

Chang Mei-hui 張美惠 . 'Ming-tai chung-kuo jen tsai Hsien-lo chih mao-i' 明代中國人在暹羅之貿易 (Chinese Traders in Siam during the Ming Dynasty), *Wen-shih-che hsüeh-pao* 文史哲學報 , No.3 (1951) pp.161-176.

Chang Wei-hua 張維華 . *Meng-tai hai-wai mao-i chien-lun* 明代海外貿易簡論 (A Brief Discussion on Ming's Oversea Trade) Shanghai, 1955.
Ming-shih Fu-land-chi lu-sung ho-lang I-ta-li-ya shih-chüan chu-hsi 明史佛郎機和蘭意大利亞四傳注釋 (Annotation of the Portuguese, the Spanish, the Dutch, the Italian in *Ming History*), Yenching Journal of Chinese Studies Monograph Series, No.7, (Peking) 1934.

Ch'ao-chou fu-chi 潮州府志 (Prefectural Gazetteer of Ch'ao-chou). Comp. by Chou Shih-hsün 周碩勳 . 44 *chüan*, 1762.

Ch'ao-yang hsien-shih 潮陽縣志 (Country Gazetteer of Ch'ao-yang). Comp. by Chou Heng-chung. 23 *chüan*, 1884.

Chen Ching-ho 陳荆和 . 'Ch'ing-chu hua-po chi Changchi mao-i' 清初 (The Chinese junk trade in Nagasaki in early Chi'ng), *Nanyang Hsüeh-pao*, Vol.9.

Chen Yü-shung 陳育崧. 'Hsin-chia-po Hua-wen pei-ming chi-lu hsi-yen' 新加坡華文碑銘集錄緒言(Preface to the Chinese tablets in Singapore), *Nanyang Hsüeh-pao*, Vol.26, 1971. 南洋學報

'Hsü shih-la ku-chi' 字石叻古蹟 (Preface to the Historical Relics in Singapore), *Shih-la ku-chi*, Singapore 1975.

Chen Tse-hsien 陳澤憲. 'Shih-chiu shi-chi te chi-yüeh lao-kung chih-tu' 十九世紀契約華工制度 (The Ticket System in the 19th Century), *Li-shih Yen-chiu*, I 1963.

Cheng Shih kuan-hsi wen-shu 鄭氏關係文書 . (Documents in Relation with the Cheng family), Taiwan wen Hsien Ts'ung K'an, ti 69 Chung. Taiwan, 1960.

Chia-ying chou-chih 嘉應州志 (Prefectural Gazetteer of Chia-ying). Comp. by Wen Chung-wen 溫仲文 , 32 chüan 1898.

Chieh-yang hsien-chih 揭陽縣志 (Country Gazetter of Chia-ying). Comp. by Liu Yeh-ch'in, 劉業勤 9 chüan, 1779.

Chou Hsüan-wei 周玄暐. *Chien-lin shü-chi* 涇林續紀 , *Han-fen lou mi-chi* 涵芬樓秘笈 , chi 8 Fen Puei (also Wan Puei in some other sources) 'hai-k'ou I-chien' 海寇議前 (Discussion on Piracy) *Hsuan lan-tang ch'ung shu hsu-chi*, 玄覽堂叢書續集 Vol.15.

Chü Ta-chin 屈大鈞 . *Kwangtung Hsin-yu* 廣東新語 (New Discussion on Kwangtung), 28 chüan, 1974, Hong Kong.

Chu Yüo 朱或 . *Ping-chou k'o tan* 萍洲可談 3 chüan, Taiwan 1975.

Chung-kuo chin-shan-pai-lien she-wei chin-chi Shih-lun-chi 中國近三百年社會經濟史論集 (A Symposium on the Socio-economic History of China of the Last Three Centuries), 4 vols., Hong Kong, 1974.

Chung-kuo chin-tai shou-kung-yeh shih tzu-liao 中國近代手工業史資料 (Materials of the Modern History of the Chinese Handicrafts), Comp. by Peng tse-I, Peking, 1957.

Chung-kuo tzu-pen chu-yi meng-ya wen-ti tao-lun chi 中國資本主義萌芽問題討論集 (A symposium on the problems of the sprout of Chinese capitalism), Peking, 1957.

Fu-chien t'ung-chi 福建通志 (Provincial Gazetter of Fukien). Comp. by Ch'en shou-chi 陳壽祺 , 284 *chüan* 1868.

Fu I-ling 傅衣凌 . *Ming-Ch'ing Shih-tai Shan-jen Chi Shang-yeh tzu-pen* 明清時代商人及商業資本 (Merchants and Mercantile Capital in Ming and Ch'ing Times), Peking 1956.

Han Huai-chun 韓槐準 . 'Ta-po-kung kao' 大伯公考 (Investigation on the Origins of the Worship of Ta-po-kung) *Nanyang Hsüeh-pao*, vol. 1, pt. 2.

Hsia-men chih 厦門志 (Gazetter of Amoy). Comp. by Chou K'ai 周凱 , 16 *chüan* 1832.

Hsiao-fang hu-chai yü-ti ts'ung-ch'ao 小方壺齋輿地叢鈔 (Collected Texts on Geography from the Hsiao-fang hu Studio) Comp. by Wang Hsi-ch'i 王錫祺 , 1887-1897.

Hsieh Ch'ing-kao 謝清高 . *Hai-lu* 海錄 (A Maritime Record). 2 *chüan* 1842.

Hsü Chi-yü 徐継畬 . *Ying-huan chih-lüeh* 瀛環志略 (A Brief Discussion of the Ocean Circuit) 10 *chüan*, 1850.

Huang-ch'ao ching-shih wen-pien 皇朝經世文編 (Essays on Statecraft during the Ch'ing Dynasty). Comp. by Ho Ch'ang-ling 賀長齡 , 120 *chüan* 1873.

Hui-chou fu-chi 惠州府志 (Prefectural Gazetteer of Hui-chou) Comp. by Liu Kuei-lien 46 *chüan* 1881.

Hung chiu-lu 鴻猷錄

Ishihara Michihiro 石原道博 . 'Cheng chi-lung No Nihon Nankai Boeki' 鄭芝龍の日本南海貿易 (Cheng Chih-lung's Overseas Trade in Japan and Southeast Asia) *Minami Asia Gakuho*, No.1.

Iwao Seiichi 岩生成一 . 'Kinse Shoki Taigai Kankei' 近世初期對外關係 (Japan's Foreign Relations in Early Modern Period) *Iwanami Koza, Nihon Rekishi* 15 岩波講座日本歴史 .

Kobata Atsuhi 小葉田淳 . 'Medai Chang-chou Union-chou jin no Kaigai Shogyo Hatten' 明代漳泉人の海外商業發展 (Chang-chou Merchants in Ming's Overseas Trade) *Tao Ronso, Vol. 4, 1942. Chusei Nichu Koutsu Boekishi No Kenkyu.*

Kuan Lü-chüan 關履權 . 'Sung-tai Kwangtung chi hsiang-liao mao-i' 宋代廣東之香料貿易 (The Spice Trade in Sung Canton), *SLC*, Vol.2.

Kuang Kuo-hsiang 鄺國祥 'Ping-lang-i hai-chuo-i Ta-po-kung' 梹郎嶼海珠嶼大伯公 (Notes on Tapokung in Penang) *Nanyang hsüeh-pao*, Vol.9, pt.1.

Lai Yung-hsiang 賴永祥 ed. *Ming Cheng yen-chiu ts'ung-chi* 明鄭研究叢刊 (Collected Studies on the Cheng Family of the Ming), 3 vols. Taipei, 1953,1954,1955.

Liang T'ing-nan 梁廷枏 ed. *Yueh-hai-kuan chih* 粵海關志 (Gazetteer of Kwangtung Maritime Customs), c.1839.

Li Chien-nung 李劍農. *Sung-yuan-Ming chin-chi-shih kao* 宋元明經濟史稿 (A Draft of the Economic History of the Sung Yüan Ming Dynasties) Peking, 1957.

Li Lung-chien 李龍潛. 'Yeh chung-liu yi Teng Mao-chi ch'i-i te terh-chen' 葉宗留鄧茂七起義的特徵 (The Characteristics of the Uprising of Yeh Chung-liu and Teng Mao-chi) *Li-shih chiao-hsüeh* Peking, 1957, No.3.

Li Yao 李瑤. *I-shih shih-i* 繹史拾遺 (Supplement to the Complete History) Taiwan Yin Hang Chin Chi Ying Chiu Shih: Taiwan wen Hsien ti 132 Chung, Taiwan, 1962.

Lin Hsiao-sheng 林孝勝, *et.al. Shih-la ku-chi* 石叻古蹟 (Historical Relics in Singapore), Singapore 1975.

Lo hsiang-lin 羅香林. *K'o-chai shih-liao hui-pien* 客家史料滙編 (A Collection of Historical Sources on the Hakka), Hong Kong, 1965.
Hsi-po-lo-chou lo-fang-po teng shou chien kung-ho-kuo kao (A Historical Survey of the Lan-fang Presidential System in West Borneo) Hong Kong, 1961. 西婆羅洲羅芳伯等所建共和國考

Lü Chen-yü 呂振羽. *Chien-ming chung-kuo tung-shih* 簡明中國通史 (A Concise History of China) Peking, 1956.

Ming-ch'ing shih-liao I-pien 明清史料乙編 (Historical Materials of the Ming and Ch'ing. Series B.) Shanghai, 1936 ed.

Ming-ch'ing shih-liao tin-pien 明清史料丁編 (Historical Materials of the Ming and Ch'ing. Series D.) Taiwan 1972 ed.

Ming-shih 明史 (History of Ming) 332 *chüan* 1678-1739. Shanghai, 1916 ed.

Ming Yin-chung shih-lu 明英宗實錄 (The Veritable Record of Ming Yin-chung Emperor).

Ming-shih chi-shih pen-mo 明史紀事本末 (Chronological Account of the Ming). 80 chüan, Shanghai, 1939 ed.

Shen Yün 沈雲 . *T'ai-wan Cheng-shih shih-mo* 台灣鄭氏始末 (Complete Record of the Cheng Family of Taiwan), Taiwan Yin hang Ching chiyen chiu shih, Taiwan wen hsien t'sung k'an ti 15 chung.

Shih-liao shün-k'ang 史料旬刊 (Seasonal Publication of Historical Materials) Taiwan rep. 1963.

Tai-ping T'ien-kuo chi-yi t'iao-cha pao-kao 太平天國起義調查報告 (Report of the Finding of Taiping), Peking, 1956.

Tanaka, M. 田中正俊 *To Moshichi no ran no shoden ni tsuite* (On the Historical Records Concerning the Rebellion of Teng Mao-chi) *Mindaishi Ronso*, Tokyo, 1962.

T'an Tsui 檀萃 . *Tien-hai-Yü Heng chih* 滇海虞衡志 (Record of Yünnan) 13 chüan *Wen-yü-lou yü-ti ts'ung-shu* 問影樓叢書 Book 5.

Tatsuro Yamamoto 山本達郎 *Betonamu Chugoku kankei shi.* バトナム中國關係史 (History of International Relations Between Vietnam and China), Tokyo, 1975.

T'ien Ju-k'ang 田汝康 . *Shih-ch'i shih-chi chih shih-chiu shih-chi chung-yeh chung-kuo fan-ch'uan tsai tung-nan ya-chou hang-yün ho shang-yeh shang te ti-wei* 十七世紀及十九世紀中葉中國航船在東南亞洲航運和商業上的地位 (The Place of Chinese Sailing Ships in the Maritime Trade of Southeast Asia from the 17th to the mid-19th centuries) *CKSS*, Vol.4.

Ura Ken'ichi 浦廉一 . 'Yen-p'ing-wang hu-kuan Cheng Tai Ch'ang-ch'i ts'un-yin chih yen-chiu' 延平王戶官鄭泰存銀長崎研究 (A Study of the Silver Kept in Nagasaki by Cheng T'ai, Cheng Ch'eng-kung's financial official). *T'ai-wan feng-wu* 台灣風物 (The Taiwan Folkways), 11.3:25-150 (March, 1961).
唐船風說書研究 *Karafune fusetsusho no kenkyu* (A Study Concerning Chinese junks) *Kai hentai* 華夷變態 , Tokyo, 1958.

Wang Chia-chien. 王家儉 *Wei Yüan tuei hsi-fan tse jen-shih chi-chi hai-fan shi-hsiang* 魏源對西方的認識及其海防思想 (Wei Yüan, His concept on the Maritime Defence and his Understanding of the West), Taipei, 1964.

Wang Shih-chen 王士禎 & Hsia Tse-yang 夏子陽 . *Shih Liu-ch'iu lu* 使琉球錄 (The Mission to Liu-ch'iu) Taipei rep. 1962.

Wei Yüan 魏源 . *Hai-kuo t'u-chih* 海國圖志 (An Illustrated Treatise on the Maritime Kingdoms). 60 *chüan* 1847.

Wen-tai Wo-tsuan 虔台倭纂 (Collected Materials on Japanese Piracy) Vol.1 *Hsüan Lan-tang ch'ung shu hsu-chi* 玄覽堂叢書續集 Vol.17.

Wu Fa 吳法 . *T'ai-wan Liu-shih cha-chi* 台灣歷史札記 (Notes on the History of Taiwan) Hong Kong, 1976.

Yamawaki Daijiro 山脇悌次郎 . *Nagasaki no To-jin boeki* 長崎の唐人貿易 (Chinese Trade in Nagasaki). Tokyo, 1964.

Yang Ying 楊英 . *Ts'ung-cheng chih-lu* 從征實錄 (Record of Following of Campaigns of Ch'eng Ch'eng-kung). Tai-wan Ying hang. Ching Chi yen Chiu Shih. Tai-wan wen hsien t'sung k'an, ti 32 chung. Taiwan, 1958.

Yen Chung-p'ing 嚴中平 . *Ch'ing-tai Yün-nan tung-cheng kao* 清代雲南銅政考 (A Study of Yünnan Copper Mining). Shanghai, 1948.

Yuan Yuan. *Yün-nan t'ung chih-kao* 雲南通志稿 (A General Gazetteer of Yünnan) 1835.

WESTERN LANGUAGE SOURCES

Anon., 1878-1879. 'The Chinese in Borneo', *The China Review*, Hong Kong, Vol.VII, pp.1-11.

Bezemer, T.J., *Beknopte Encyclopaedië van Nederlandsch Oost-Indië*, Leiden, 1921

Boxer, C.R. 'The Rise and Fall of Nicholas Iquan', *T'ien-hsia Monthly*, 11.5:401-439.
ed. and tr. *South China in the 16th Century*, Hakluyt Society, wer.2, Vol.106, London, 1953.

Cator, W.J., 1936. *The Economic Position of the Chinese in Netherlands Indies*, Oxford.

Crawfurd, J., 1820. *History of the Indian Archipelago*, Edinburgh, 3 vols.
Journal of an Embassy to the Court of Siam and Cochin China, Kuala Lumpur, 1967. Originally published in 1828.

Cushman, J.W. *Fields From the Seas: Chinese Junk Trade with Siam during the late 18th and early 19th Centuries, Ph.D. Thesis, Cornell University, June, 1975. (Unpublished).*

Dagh-register gehouden in 't Casteel Batavia, 1628-1682. 31 vols. Batavia.

Doty, E, and Pohlman, W.J., 'Tour in Borneo, from Sambas through Montrado to Pontianak, and the adjacent settlements of Chinese and Dayaks, during the autumn of 1838', *Chinese Repository* (Canton), Vol.VIII, No.6, pp.283-310.

Earl, G.W., 1837. *The Eastern Seas*, London.

Elvin, Mark. *The Pattern of the Chinese Past*, New York, 1973.

Francis, E.A., 1842. 'Westkust van Borneo in 1832', Tijdschrift voor Nederlandsch-Indië, Vol.LI, pp.241-262.

Generale Missiven Der V.O.C. Deel I, (1610-1638).

Groot, J.J., 1885. *Het Kongsiwezen van Borneo. Eene verhandeling over den Grondslag en den Aard der Chineesche Politieke Vereeniginen in de Koloniën, met eene Chineesche Geschiedenis van de Kongsi Lanfang,* 's-Gravenhage.

Gutzlaff, C., *Journal of Three Voyages*, London, 1839.

Ho Ping-ti., *The Ladder of Success in Imperial China*, New York, 1962.

Hunt, J., 1812. 'Sketch of Borneo, or Pulo Kalamantan' in Keppel, 1847, Vol.1. Appendix V, pp.382-429.

Irwin, G., 1955. *Nineteenth-Century Borneo: A Study in Diplomatic Rivalry*, Singapore.

Iwao Seiichi, ed. *Shih-ch'i shih-chi T'ai-wan Ying-kuo mao-i shih-liao* 十七世紀台灣英國貿易史料 (Sources on English Trade with Taiwan in the 17th century). *T'ai-wan yen-chiu ts'ung-k'an* 台灣研究叢刊 (Collection of Studies on Taiwan), No.57. Taipei, 1959.
'Li Tan, Chief of the Chinese Residents at Hirado, Japan in the Last Days of the Ming Dynasty'. *Memoir of Research Department of the Tokyo Bunko* 17:27-83 (1958).

Jackson, J.C., *Chinese in the West Borneo Goldfields: A Study in Cultural Geography*, London, 1970.

Keppel, H., 1847. *The Expedition to Borneo of H.M.S. Dido*, London, 2 Vols.

Kierman, F.A. and Fairbank, J.K., ed. *Chinese Ways in Warfare*, New York, 1974.

Logan, J.P., 1847. 'The Present Condition of the Indian Archipelago', *Journal Ind. Arch.*
'Notices of the Chinese Intercourse with Borneo', *Journal Ind. Arch.* 1848, pp.611-15.

Melink-Roelofsz, M.A.P. *Asia Trade and European Influence in the Indonesian Archipelago between 1500 and about 1630.* The Hague: Martinus Mijhoff, 1962.

Moor, J.H., 1837. (ed.), *Notices of the Indian Archipelago and Adjacent Countries...* Singapore.

Myers, Pamon H., 'Some Issues on Economic Organization During the Ming and Ch'ing Periods: A Review Article' *Ch'ing-shih Wen-ti* 清史問題 , (Problems of Ch'ing History), No.2 (December 1974), pp.77-95.

Peng, Chang. *The Distribution and Relative Strength of the Proverbial Merchant Groups in China, 1842-1911*, Ph.D. Thesis, University of Washington (1957), unpublished.

Posewitz, T., 1892. *Borneo: Its Geology and Mineral Resources*, London.

Purcell, V., *The Chinese in Southeast Asia*, London, 1952, 1965.

Rees, W.A. van, Montrado. *Geschied- en krijgkundige bijdrage betreffende de onderwerping der Chinesen op Borneo*, 's-Hertigenbosch, Muller, 1858.

Schaannk, S.H., 1893. 'De Kongsi'd van Montrado ... ' Tijdschrift voor Indische Taal-, Land-, en Volkenkunde, Vol.XXXV, Nos.5 and 6, pp.498-612.

Shiba, Yoshinobu, *Commerce and Society in Sung China*, Mark Elvin tr., New York, 1970.

So Kwan-wai, *Japanese Piracy in Ming China during the 16th Century*, New York, 1975.

Somers Heidhues, H.F., *Southeast Asia's Chinese Minorities*, London, 1974.

Straits Settlements Blue Books and Returns of Imports and Exports, 1870-1915.

Temminck, C.J., 1947. *Coup-d'oel Générdal sur les Possesions Neerlandaises dans Lólnde Archipélagique*, Leiden, Vol.2.

T'ien Ju-kang, 1953. *The Chinese of Sarawak: A Study of Social Structure*, (London School of Economics Monographs on Social Anthropology, No.12).

Veth, P.J., 1854-56. *Borneo's Wester-afdeeling, ...* Zaltbommel, 2 vols.

Wang Gungwu, 'The Origins of Civilization: An Essay on Chinese Scholarship at transition' forthcoming 4th issue of *Asian Thought and Society*, 1977.

Ward, B.E., 1954. 'A Hakka Kongsi in Borneo', *Journal of Oriental Studies*, Vol.1, pp.358-370.

Wong Lin-ken, 1965. *The Malayan Tin Industry to 1914*, Tucson, Arizona.

INDEX

A sure way of self-motivation through constant exposure of auspicious symbols

SECRETS OF ANCIENT CHINESE ART OF MOTIVATION

Dr. Ong Hean-Tatt
ISBN 967 978 464 9

SECRETS OF ANCIENT CHINESE ART OF MOTIVATION highlights the principles of success and management for business, marriage, family, nation building and even war. This is a practical, adaptable book for all situations. It reveals not only the secret of effective relationship within an organization but also the essential canon leading to family unity and harmony.

Each chapter is developed to show the parts of the fundamental doctrine which has been tested for centuries by the ancient masters.

Without appropriate strategies to influence or motivate, there would be no satisfying accomplishment in the long run. The great secret is the use of powerful symbols to favour industry and the desire towards greater achievements and affluence.

Dr. Ong Hean-Tatt is also the author of two other notable books on Chinese Studies — THE CHINESE PAKUA and CHINESE ANIMAL SYMBOLISMS. Both focus on the foundation of Chinese culture and logic.